THE TEACHER'S GUIDE TO HELPING YOUNG CHILDREN GROW

The Teacher's Manual

THE TEACHER'S GUIDE TO HELPING YOUNG CHILDREN GROW

The Teacher's Manual

ERNA FURMAN

INTERNATIONAL UNIVERSITIES PRESS, INC.

Madison

Connecticut

Library of Congress Cataloging-in-Publication Data

Furman, Erna.

Teachers guide to helping young children grow.

Bibliography: p.
Includes index.
1. Child development—Study and teaching.
I. Furman, Erna.   Helping young children grow.
II. Title.
HQ767.9.F87   1987 Suppl.   305   87-3197
ISBN 0-8236-2275-4

Contents

1

How This Study Came to Be

This study has its roots in thirty years of research and teaching by members of the Cleveland Center for Research in Child Development. We serve children of varied religious, ethnic, and racial backgrounds, rich and poor, helping them to resolve their emotional troubles. Our data are gathered from ongoing observations of and work with young children and their parents in the Hanna Perkins Therapeutic Nursery School and Kindergarten (R. A. Furman and Katan, 1969), and from the five times weekly individual psychoanalytic treatments of children of all ages in our Child Analytic Clinic. Our team of specialists in child development, educators, and child psychoanalysts devotes thousands of hours to the detailed study, understanding, and service of each of these youngsters and their families. All of them are seen over periods of several years and most are followed up at intervals. Their personal benefits, however, are but one aspect of our endeavor. During research meetings, chaired by our psychiatric directors, Drs. A. Katan and R. A. Furman, and in special project study groups, we scrutinize and compare the hard-won insights, and use the knowledge gained from the work with individual cases to understand how personalities develop, to pinpoint significant factors which facilitate or hinder healthy growth, and to devise practical educational measures for the prevention of emotional illness. Through publications and teaching we acquaint professionals and parents with our findings and help the wider community to apply them toward furthering the healthy development of many more children than we can work with ourselves. Our students, in turn, teach us, by sharing their experiences, ideas, and questions, and by alerting us to their interests and needs (E. Furman, 1980, 1981, 1984, 1986). They have also helped us to understand better the process of learning about child development and to improve our methods of teaching it.

From this mutually instructive endeavor grew the demand for a comprehensive book on child development. The impetus for writing it came when we had to use our accumulated knowledge and experience to tackle a new challenge. In 1973, Judge Mary Conway Kohler of the National Commission on Resources for Youth asked our Center to develop a parent preparation course for teenagers. Judge Kohler's request touched a responsive chord in us. We knew of the recently initiated massive effort of the U.S. Department of Health, Education and Welfare's (HEW) Office of Education to improve the competence of teenagers as prospective parents. Our own professional and personal experiences had already alerted us to many young people's wish to understand emotional growth and to apply it to their work as sitters, tutors, or counselors. Adolescence is a time of "getting it together" as an adult, a period when the parental model is carefully scrutinized, and when additional concepts about child care may be sought and accepted. We did not intend to address the older adolescent as a prospective parent but hoped that knowledge and understanding integrated at this time would helpfully contribute to future parenting skills.

In 1974, six members of our Center formed a study group to address the task. The participants were Elizabeth Daunton, Eleanor Fiedler, Robert A. Furman, M.D., Joan Rich, Ph.D., Arthur L. Rosenbaum, M.D., and myself. All of us were child psychoanalysts and taught courses in child development, but our training and experience also included related disciplines: Three of us were qualified teachers with classroom experience in high schools, one was a pediatrician, one a social worker, two were psychologists, two were psychoanalysts of adults, and four were currently parents of adolescents. A fuller account of our group's work is contained in the subsequent chapters, but a brief synopsis is in order here to show how our thinking and experience led to the writing of the book itself and the accompanying Guide.

During the first two years of research, the study group's efforts focused on developing a syllabus which would meet the needs of young people in late adolescence. We aimed to include all the vital areas of personality growth in childhood, to present them in the manner and sequence which we had come to appreciate as most helpful to learners, and to fit them into the format and curriculum of a senior high school. We then refined and adapted this course outline in the light of actual teaching experience, when members of our group taught it in three consecutive senior classes at a local public high school. This pilot work proved so successful that we moved on to our next goal, to train several interested and gifted teachers who wished to, and eventually did, take over the teaching of the course at their schools. The teachers were Penny Friedman and Theodore Wiehe, from the Social Science Department of the Shaker Heights High School, and Carl Tuss and Marilyn Machlup, principal and assistant principal of the School on Magnolia. Their course with me began in 1978 and followed the exact same syllabus and technique as the students. It was assisted and recorded by Dr. Rich and closely monitored by the study group. It proved so well suited to the needs and interests of the teachers and was so much appreciated by them that we began to use it with other lay and professional groups. During this time also, the newly trained teachers' own teaching of child development in their senior high school classes got under way, helped by our ongoing discussions of their practical experiences. Close scrutiny of all the teaching experiences and related research records indicated that this course in child development was indeed geared to people of all ages and levels of sophistication. How had this happened?

To devise a curriculum for late adolescents, we did not "water down" the available body of knowledge, but distilled its essence, focusing on basic concepts of personality growth, and arranging them in internally coherent sequences. We avoided scientific terms and theory, and dealt with practical situations. The teaching method, designed to suit the subject and to facilitate learning, proved adaptable to varied settings and class sizes. It consisted mainly of discussion seminars where students work with the teacher and participate actively, contributing their observations, questions, and thoughts. This approach addresses the inherent strengths in all learners, engages their feeling, thinking, and experience, and helps them to integrate and apply knowledge in their daily lives, regardless of intellectual acumen or expertise. Thus, whereas at the start we had applied our experiences with teaching professionals and adult laymen to working with late adolescents, in the end the process was reversed. Teaching high school students taught us how to work better with other groups, and enabled us to develop a syllabus and refine a method appropriate and helpful to all.

To some of us this came as a surprise, to others not. Dr. Rich, in particular, had hoped all along that our efforts would bear such fruit. It now became necessary to gather and detail our findings in order to share them with others interested in learning and teaching child development. Our goals were: (1) to present the subject matter (i.e. the syllabus on personality growth in childhood), in a manner that would approximate the give and take of joint work in class discussions and to include in it the many areas of interest which had emerged in the process of teaching; (2) to discuss and illustrate our method of teaching and experiences with it; (3) to relate how its techniques were adapted for use with varied groups of learners in different settings, and with varying size and duration of classes; (4) to describe how teachers were trained to teach this course themselves. It ultimately seemed best to reserve the book itself for the subject matter and to include the other topics in this Guide.

The writing became my task. I utilized our records of the work of the study group, of the meetings and discussions with the teachers, of the class sessions, of individual students' progress, and of the hundreds of oral and written questions and responses of all the learners, young and old. As in teaching, I also drew on the available body of knowledge about child development, especially on the findings and experiences of our research team at the Cleveland Center for Research in Child Development and the Hanna Perkins School. As chapters were completed, the teachers used them in their work with high school seniors, parents, and professionals. Their comments and experiences with the material helped to modify and expand it. By the end of 1983, close to two thousand students had taken the course and contributed to it. The study group had by then ceased to meet but members were kept in touch with progress. Dr. Robert A. Furman studied all chapters, made many suggestions, and lent moral support. I needed it. The work was arduous. Many concepts and terms had to be newly worded in colloquial language and linked with clinical vignettes, disguised only to assure confidentiality. Several areas of the subject matter had to be freshly thought through and formulated. Data from the teaching experiences had to be evaluated and interpreted.

Although I accept sole responsibility for what I wrote, I feel deeply grateful and indebted to my colleagues, especially the members of the study group, to the teachers who learned and worked with us enthusiastically, to Dr. Robert A. Furman who helped in so many capacities. And I thank the many students who participated in our courses. To them I also owe the subtitle, "I Never Knew Parents Did So Much," the phrase they used most often in their spontaneous comments to express what they had learned.

Throughout the years of study and writing only the child analysts' teaching sessions and related secretarial expenses were reimbursed. For that we are grateful to Dr. M. Freeman of the Shaker Heights Board of Education, the Martha Holden Jennings Foundation, and the Cleveland Center for Research in Child Development.

2

What it Takes to Learn Child Development

THE CHOICE OF METHOD

Earlier I described how the study group utilized our experiences in clinical work, research, and teaching to select and arrange the content of the child development syllabus: to determine *what* should be taught and learned. All along, we focused equal attention on the method best suited to this subject: *how* it can be taught and learned. In thinking about this latter aspect our group initially also drew on past experience which, as I related before, had led us to adopt a certain approach. It consisted of using the Socratic method, in which the teacher helps the student to explore and develop his own thinking, adding new facts selectively when gaps in knowledge have been pinpointed and more information is sought, and gradually contrasting and linking old and new understanding, to the extent and at the pace set by the individual student.

How had we reached this conclusion? Over many years, all of us had taught child development in many ways, in many settings, and with many students. We had repeatedly evaluated and compared these experiences, and adapted and refined our approach accordingly. By the time we undertook the task of this child development course, we had found that the method described here is psychologically the most sound and works best in practice. We used it with hundreds of professionals in the fields of health and education, in groups and individually. We worked with pediatricians, medical students, residents and teaching fellows in child psychiatry, social workers, psychologists, psychotherapists, nursery school, elementary school and high school teachers, day care workers, staff in children's institutions and residential treatment centers, and child life workers in hospitals. We also worked with parents of children of all ages, especially with parents of young children. Usually groups of four to fifteen students met for one or one-and-a-half hours in weekly or biweekly seminars with their psychoanalytically trained specialist in child development. The courses were mostly designed for one year. Many participants, however, found their learning so rewarding that they wanted to increase and deepen their understanding further and therefore attended extended courses for several years. Although our experience in this area may be the most extensive and intensive, it is not unique. Anna Freud and her co-workers taught child development by this method as early as the 1920s (E. Furman, 1978). Since that time, she and others have worked in similar form with lay and professional groups in Europe and in this country. In 1979, the method and its results were validated formally. Taking as its subjects nursery school teachers who had participated in our courses, this independent research project confirmed the positive impression we had gained informally (Redmond, 1979).

Since this method offered optimal benefits, all members of our study group were agreed on the need to use it in our planned course, although we were well aware of the difficulties and limitations it entailed. Our task now was to apply and use it effectively with students of different ages, backgrounds, and interests, in settings with different class sizes, time limits, and learning environments.

During the first year of our monthly research meetings we studied these questions with the help of data from our prior teaching experiences. Later, when we were working out practical arrangements to include the course in the curriculum of specific schools, we addressed the problems of applying our findings and fitting them in with the requirements of these settings. Once the course actually got under way, we closely followed and discussed the teaching and learning experiences gained during three consecutive full-length courses for senior high school students, one taught by Dr.

Robert A. Furman, two by myself. For this purpose the study group availed themselves of the students' weekly written assignments as well as of the teachers' detailed records of all aspects of the oral class work. Both types of data were subsequently indexed in such a way as to allow topics of interest to emerge and to assist us in researching various facets. Among these were each student's approach to learning, ease or difficulty in utilizing the method, and in mastering and applying concepts; responses to different aspects of the subject matter, to the teacher and to peers; direct and indirect questions and contributions, the student's own and the teacher's evaluations of what was learned; the many-sided role of the teacher, of the teacher–pupil relationships; and difficulties encountered in teaching, handling of students' personal remarks and requests, of class situations, and of external events which affected the learning environments. When the child development course was later taught to a small group of teachers, the study group similarly followed, compared, and evaluated these experiences.

Many insights and adaptations of method resulted from the study group's concentrated effort. These were further extended and deepened during the following five years of work with the newly trained teachers. By that time the research group no longer met, but my regular meetings with the teachers, assisted by Dr. Joan Rich, provided an ongoing opportunity for learning. We utilized the data from fifty-four child development courses taught at the Shaker Heights High School, a large public school where twenty to thirty-two students attended each class, and from five child development courses taught at the School on Magnolia, a small private school, where three to six students attended each class. This comprised in all about 1,600 senior high school students. In addition, we accumulated data from about one hundred and fifty students of different age groups, backgrounds, and settings as, during these years, the child development course was also taught to groups of parents, educators, mental health professionals, and pediatricians.*

The conclusions and formulations presented here derive

---

*Since the time of this writing, over two thousand more high school seniors have taken the child development course as well as many more groups of adults.

from all these observations and experiences and owe a great deal to the thinking contributed by the members of the research group and teaching staff.

Teaching and learning are a cooperative undertaking, focused on a common goal. Teacher and student agree to work toward it together. The task is always demanding of both partners, but especially so with this particular method and subject matter. Our deliberations focused first on what the students need to contribute and the special difficulties they need to cope with.

We had carefully considered introducing the child development course to a yet younger age group, but anticipated that they would not yet have reached the phase of personality integration which provides this healthy developmental motivation and related capacity to utilize the material. This proved to be the case in practice, when a class of fourteen and fifteen-year-olds was taught at the School on Magnolia and when a few younger and emotionally less mature students participated in classes at the Shaker Heights High School. Some of these students were not sufficiently interested, others had difficulty in addressing the concepts thoughtfully and in applying them constructively.

However, we also knew that age and emotional maturity are not the only factors. Personalities vary. Neither the developmental motivations nor those related to work and parenting are always present. Some parents and professionals who work with children are not interested in learning about child development and we expected this to be equally true of older teenagers and young adults. For this reason, we felt from the start that courses in child development should be elective. We still maintain this opinion, although many of our students (and many administrators) insist that such courses should be mandatory for all potential or prospective parents and for all who are engaged in the care of children. We find it helpful for students to know ahead of time what the course is about, through a written description and/or discussion with the teacher, and to have the choice of enrolling in it or of signing up for another course with equal credits if the setting, such as a high school, has credit requirements.

Although the developmental processes and the perhaps vaguely felt wish to understand oneself and one's interactions with others, generally stimulate a healthy interest, they also have potential drawbacks in that they may foster excessive and unproductive introspection. When young people find themselves bewildered and distressed by their mental growing pains (or when older people experience personal difficulties), they sometimes hope that learning about child development will aid them in dealing with their own troubles. Consciously or unconsciously, they then focus on themselves and on their relationships as subjects of observation and application. It can only result in neither understanding their own difficulties nor learning child development. Our study group rightly felt that this unhelpful tendency, which has to be reckoned with at several different points in teaching child development, would be considerably minimized if the students, like the professionals and parents, had ongoing contact with children and an opportunity to observe them. This helps to direct the learner's attention to youngsters whose personalities function at a different stage of development from their own. It does not mean that the student will, or indeed should, leave himself and his experiences out of his learning, but it will help him to consider available memories of the past, rather than current concerns, and to relate them to what he learns and observes in children, instead of focusing on them as an end in itself.

OBSERVING CHILDREN

Observation of children is not merely a way of counteracting unhelpful introspection. It is an essential part of the student's learning process. What real individual children do and say helps us to understand them, to form general ideas about the ways in which their personalities grow and function, to test and refine our knowledge, and put it to practical use. When general ideas are not linked to observational data, a discussion of them readily turns into pseudophilosophical polemics based on personal opinions. Adolescents especially, and all of us at times, are prone to indulge in subjective theorizing which serves as an end in itself, far from the paths of scientific endeavor.

With these considerations in mind, we initially thought

that all participating students should be required to engage in work with children during their attendance of the course. In practice this is extremely difficult to arrange. A survey showed that some senior high school students do hold jobs in child care, that many more have done so in the recent past, and that all have some opportunity to observe children in families or in the community, at least in stores and on the street. We decided to alert students who signed up for the course that ongoing work with children, or opportunity to observe them, is most desirable. In one of the schools we were able to offer a limited number of volunteer jobs at an adjacent elementary school to be undertaken during the lunch hour.

THE STUDENTS' MOTIVATION

The student, above all, needs to want to learn. Something must motivate him or her to study child development. The professionals and parents we had mostly worked with were highly motivated. They hoped to gain greater knowledge and better understanding of child development in order to apply it effectively in their professional or parenting work with children. They were in ongoing contact with children, shouldering responsibility for some or all aspects of their healthy growth and upbringing, taking care of them. They wanted to do their job well and wanted to master the situations which puzzled them or frustrated their efforts. However, many of them also later commented that their learning had not only helped their understanding and handling of children, but had also benefited their professional growth and had especially enhanced their appreciation of parenthood, in themselves and in others. The comment "I never knew parents did so much" was voiced as often by them as it was by the high school seniors and young adults. It was phrased in many ways, such as, "I never knew my parents did so much," or "I never realized that even the parents of difficult children did so many good things for them," and it often cropped up as "I never knew *I* did so much as a parent." This does not mean that their studies served a personal therapeutic purpose. It merely suggests that subsidiary motives had contributed to their wish to learn about child development and that they were able to select and integrate some of it in these areas of their functioning.

With young people in their late teens and early twenties, the motives for learning child development differ. Those who work part-time with youngsters (as sitters, tutors, counselors) encounter sufficient difficulties and frustrations in their handling of them to stimulate a wish for better understanding; those who consider a career may well wish to learn something about this field to help them make a good choice; and those who already are parents, even part-time parents, may seek help in raising their children. In contrast to the full-time professionals and parents, however, this work and family related motivation is usually at best of a subsidiary nature with young people, and may be absent with many. Yet we knew from our work with older teenagers and young adults and from our own children and their peers in this age group, that many had a strong interest in how personalities grow, and availed themselves of every opportunity to learn more about it.

What prompted their wish to learn? The transition from childhood into adulthood is a time when young people "get it all together," when they think about and reassess their own upbringing and inquire into the experiences of others as a part of shaping their adult personalities. It is also a time when the parental model is carefully scrutinized and when additional concepts about child care are often sought and accepted. This developmental process furnishes a special source of motivation for learning child development. Through our teaching at the high school we also found that many seniors, and some juniors, already view themselves in a potential parental role, and in some, such hitherto latent ideas are touched off by learning about child development. Our experience suggests that the mental readiness for parenthood may indeed be the most important motive in this age group.

Learning how to observe children and how to understand observations had always been an essential part of our teaching and was already included in our curriculum for this course. Even skilled professionals in ongoing contact with children always needed to learn first how to observe accurately. With the majority of high school students the difficulty proved to be not their lack of opportunity for observation but their inability to observe well and to utilize their observations in their thinking. As a result of this experience, kindling the students' interest and developing their skills in this area became an even more important focus of teaching. As they improved, they could avail themselves better of even limited opportunities for observation, and, in some cases, sought out more opportunities on their own.

DEVELOPING AND SHARING THOUGHTS AND QUESTIONS

In working with small groups of students, we had for the most part utilized class discussions in which the students developed and formulated their ideas and brought their questions. This afforded the teacher an opportunity to relate with them individually, to be in touch with their thinking, and to assist their learning. Using words is not a ready tool for everyone. Some students always found it difficult at first to express their thoughts in words but usually responded to encouragement. They learned to contribute more readily and confidently when they realized that the teacher valued their ideas and respected their way of sharing them, was willing to give them time, and did not expect sophisticated fluency. There also always were some students who talked easily but not necessarily in the service of learning and mastery. Talking may be used to control, to show off, to shock, or overwhelm others, or to provoke heated arguments. Long before the role of speech in personality development is studied as a part of the syllabus, the teacher had to be aware of its uses and misuses. Whereas some students may need to be encouraged to speak up, others may have to be asked to limit their verbal contributions at certain points. This is necessary either to allow their peers a fair share in the discussion, or because it may help our understanding to look at a topic from another angle, because a discussion takes us too far afield, or is no longer related to pertinent observations. With the teacher's alert help it was usually possible to enable everyone, or almost everyone, to participate appropriately.

Although we knew that many of the high school seniors

were neither sophisticated nor used to learning by means of discussion, we anticipated that it would be possible to assist them similarly with verbal communication. Experience proved us right, much to the surprise of the schools' other teaching staff who had feared that many students would be silent, that some would "take over," or that it would be too hard for the students to focus their thinking on the relevant issues. This does not mean that all students always participated appropriately in discussions, or that it came about without the teacher's guiding efforts. On the whole, however, class periods often seemed too short because the students were so actively involved.

What concerned us more initially was whether it would be possible to utilize this verbal discussion approach with classes of thirty or more students. With such large numbers, how would the teacher be able to maintain contact with each and know what stage they were at in their thinking? Only experience could fully answer these queries but we anticipated it by developing a helpful device—the Journal. Following each class discussion, students would be asked to write a journal which would be due before the next session. It was structured around four questions:

1. What do you remember from today's discussion?
2. Describe any experiences with children relating to it.
3. What should we discuss further?
4. What was important to you about today's discussion?

If they wished, students could write additional comments.

Experience showed that, with the help of the journal, it was possible to use our method with classes of up to thirty-two students, the largest class taught to date.* The journals served their intended purpose of extending the teacher's opportunity to get to know individual students' thinking and

---

*We did adapt our method differently, and with good results, when we taught medical students in classes of about eighty, over a period of ten years during the fifties and sixties. Each formal lecture was followed by small-group discussion periods, chaired by "their" specialist in child development. Lecturers and discussion leaders met regularly to inform each other and to coordinate teaching efforts.

responses. They made it possible for the teacher to respond to individual or personal questions in brief written comments, or with a suggestion that the student see him for a few minutes at a specified time, and thus furthered the teacher–student relationship. The journals were also good indicators of topics which had been especially difficult or were misunderstood by many so that the teacher could take them up again for further clarification and working through, and they provided an opportunity to bring to the class pertinent individual contributions or questions which had not come up in class discussion.

Moreover, the journals proved much more helpful to the students than we had expected. They afforded some an opportunity to mull over the day's session at a later time, facilitating further thinking and better integration. They enabled others to express in writing what they had been unable to verbalize in discussion. With child development, as with other subjects, some students consistently learn more readily through talking, others through writing, and others yet through a mixture of both. Thus the journal provided some with an additional or preferred means of learning. However, our experience has shown that, in child development courses, a student's means of learning does not necessarily remain consistent, nor does it serve him or her equally with all aspects of the subject matter. More often, students who are very verbal on some topics may be quite silent on others, or who write readily about some aspects cannot write about others or may find it easier to talk about them. Apparent nonlearners may "blossom out" during the course or be able to think very actively in some areas. It is therefore especially important in this course that the teacher not stereotype students in his mind but expect changes and work for them with the students through encouragement, individual discussion, and a constant attempt to understand each student's manner of learning so that one can find ways to assist him. A student's form of expression, through talking or writing, is not as indicative of his progress as the steps he takes toward mastering concepts, a topic we shall take up later.

THE RHYTHM OF LEARNING AND HOW TO UTILIZE IT
IN DIFFERENT SETTINGS

As already mentioned, our earlier courses in child development were usually designed to last one year, with one- to
one-and-a-half-hour classes at weekly or biweekly intervals.
In many instances, students then continued on in advanced
courses for several more years. This time framework had
emerged from our teaching experiences which showed that
there is an optimal rhythm in learning child development,
that the students think through the material not only during
class discussions but in the intervals between them, and that
they can integrate it better at the slower pace. The method
itself takes time to "take hold" but, once under way, works in
such a manner that the student's learning process is spontaneously ongoing and, to an extent, cyclical. Increasing
mastery is achieved by returning to topics, viewing them
from different angles, and linking them gradually with new
observations and insights to gain deeper understanding.
When the pace has not been forced and when there has been
sufficient time to learn with the teacher, students make thinking and learning about the subject their own thing. How long
it remains with them no doubt varies, but many students who
had worked with us twenty to thirty years ago commented on
how much they were still thinking about and using what they
had learned.

When we first discussed the course with the Shaker
Heights High School teachers who were interested in in-
corporating it in their curriculum, we learned that it would be
necessary to limit courses to one term, half a school year, and
that class periods lasted fifty minutes. Although the teaching
of child development would be autonomous, it would have to
be included in a course on another subject. At first this was
necessary because an independent course could not be addi-
tionally scheduled, later because neither the teachers nor
students could free up time to undertake a class which would
not meet daily. Would these limits allow sufficient time for
content and integration? We decided to keep to what we knew

was an appropriate pace, namely once weekly classes of fifty minutes, and to bow to necessity as to course length by fitting the contents into one term. The teacher would, however, have the option to curtail some portions of the content to assure sufficient discussion of others. We felt that the pace of the class should not be forced lest integration be jeopardized and result in the students' inability to assimilate any of the material. In practice some classes required more time for certain aspects and in some classes parts of the content had to be skipped, but on the whole it has proved possible to cover all of the syllabus and to see integration and mastery in process. The majority of the students who participated for one term only, felt they had got something out of the course. Perhaps they will continue thinking and learning more on their own and benefit from the aftereffect of the method as we had observed with so many others. When the child development course was later fitted into several courses on other subjects, a number of students, over the years, signed up for it a second time and learned more from this additional term of "working through." Given the high schoolers' customary quest for the new, and complaints when even a film gets a repeat showing, this indeed contrasted with their usual attitude, but was comparable to our experience with the professionals' interest in extended courses.

At the Shaker Heights High School the weekly "seminars," as the students came to call them, have been a part of social science courses in "Male/Female" (study of the changing roles of men and women in American society, past and present); in "Growth, Ageing and Dying," and "Marriage and the Family" (both are studies of customs and mores in contemporary American society); in "Criminology" (study of American crime, criminal law, and penal system—where child development partly related to how crimes, criminals, and punishments come about); and, most recently, in "Psychology" (study of several approaches to the understanding of behavior). In this last course there promises to be a first opportunity for a whole school year of consecutive weekly child development seminars.

At the School on Magnolia, child development was taught as a separate course, designed for one term but later extended to last the whole academic year at the students' request. In order to fit in with this school's lesson schedules, the teachers initially tried to teach the course daily, then three times weekly. It proved to be too fast a pace and interfered with the students' capacity to think things out for themselves and to assimilate the material. Twice weekly seminars, however, worked out quite well, but in time there too the weekly intervals were adopted.

After our experience of several years, I would still opt for one year of weekly one- to one-and-a-half-hour seminars. However, although an independent course in child development is perhaps most desirable, I would be willing to experiment with fitting it into a variety of courses on other subjects because of our interesting and successful experiences at the Shaker Heights High School. These relate in part to the teacher–pupil relationship and in part to some of the ways in which students applied what they had learned in child development to other areas.

Since our method of teaching and learning is closely tied to the teacher–pupil relationship, it is necessary for one teacher to be in charge of all communications with the students, including verbal class discussions and written exchanges via journals and comments. When the course functions as an independent entity we take this for granted. The question of another teacher then arises only in two situations—as an additional resource person or as a substitute when the class teacher is unavailable. In general it is not helpful to introduce additional resource persons or "guest speakers" on special topics. More often than not, they disrupt the continuity of the class work, deviate from its trains of thought, and interfere in the teacher–student relationship. The extra or specialized knowledge they contribute does not sufficiently counteract the adverse effects. Teacher and students are usually better off when they have to content themselves with questions left open and with details of contents remaining puzzling. However, this guideline, like most others, need not be followed rigidly. In one of his classes, for example, Mr. Wiehe invited Mrs. Machlup (both are qualified teachers of child development) at a certain point to discuss with the students her experiences in helping mothers get to know and empathize with their babies, to build a mutually satisfying relationship with them. Undoubtedly in this instance the invited guest contributed some special pertinent knowledge. The success of this session, however, was largely due to the way it was handled. Mr. Wiehe's child development course was well under way and his relationship with his students was well established before he arranged Mrs. Machlup's visit. At an earlier time in the course work, the same visit would have been confusing and difficult to integrate. He chose Mrs. Machlup because she shared his understanding of the course content and method and could be expected to respect and fit in with his class work, even though her individual style of teaching and her material would make her participation special. Mr. Wiehe also prepared the class in advance for Mrs. Machlup's session, remained in the classroom throughout, and followed it up in later discussion to assist his students with integration. His positive colleagial relationship with Mrs. Machlup no doubt not only made her participation comfortable for him but also conveyed itself helpfully to the students. In short, he spared neither means nor efforts to maximize the benefit of Mrs. Machlup's contribution and to minimize its potential hazards. This may remind the reader of the way a mother would help her young child enjoy and benefit from a first stay at a nursery school—timing geared to the child's readiness, appropriate preparation, mother remaining available, and assisting afterwards in assimilating the new impressions. It is one of the many ways in which the teacher of child development practices what he preaches or, more accurately, applies his understanding of the subject to his work with his students. By the same token, substitute teaching during the regular teacher's absence, difficult with any subject, is inadvisable in a child development course. It may be less disruptive to cancel a discussion period or to let a substitute give a lesson on a different subject than to have even a skilled but unfamiliar teacher take over, especially at short notice.

When child development is taught as an autonomous part of another subject course, the child development teacher may be the same one who teaches the other subject on the other days, or it may be a different teacher who comes in only on the assigned regular weekly seminar day. Both ways have worked out well when thoughtfully managed. When the same teacher teaches both courses, he needs to make sure that child development seminars remain regular and autonomous, and that their contents are utilized in the other subject appropriately when applicable, that they neither overwhelm it nor are kept totally isolated from it. When a different teacher teaches child development, it is helpful for the teacher of the other subject to participate in certain ways. The daily teacher accomplishes this above all by fully supporting the child development course and its teacher, by maintaining a cooperative relationship with him, by introducing the teacher to the class, and by arranging ongoing exchange of information about the students' work. If the child development teacher is new to the students, it is helpful for the daily teacher to be present, at least during the initial sessions, with or without actively taking part in the discussion. In these ways the daily teacher extends his relationship with the students to the child development course. Another avenue of participation is through sufficient interest in and understanding of its contents, so that the students' comments about it and references to it make sense, can be valued and evaluated, and so that their appropriate applications of it to the daily subject can be noted and appreciated.

At the Shaker Heights High School, where child development was always included as a part of another subject course, the teachers found repeatedly that many students applied what they learned, spontaneously and appropriately, to the other subject. They utilized both specific knowledge and newly acquired attitudes to learning, thinking, and observing. This is in part to the credit of the students, in part due to the thoughtful and skillful help of the teachers, Mrs. Friedman and Mr. Wiehe. Of course, not all subjects lend themselves to application of specific knowledge, but we were often surprised how appropriately many students linked child development to aspects of criminology, the subject we had originally viewed as the one farthest removed from child development and where the students too initially often questioned its connection with it.

These experiences suggest that the child development

course can be taught under varied "umbrellas," and that the feasibility depends to a considerable extent on the teacher and the teacher–pupil relationship.

PREPARING FOR THE CHILD DEVELOPMENT COURSE

As noted earlier, we felt that child development should be an elective rather than obligatory subject, and we also considered it important for students to know in advance about its method of teaching and learning. It needs to be emphasized from the start, even before the start, that this course differs in many respects from others, makes special and considerable demands on the students, and counts on their active participation. Students should also know who will teach the course. Since the teacher–pupil relationship is of importance and since students often know the particular teacher or have heard of him or her, this may, and should, play a part in their decision. This information has been made available to all prospective course participants in our courses, through discussion with the teacher at the time of enrollment or when students make up their schedules, and again at the beginning of the course. It is usually also described briefly in print when brochures or booklets on course selection are used.

The first child development course for senior high school students at the Shaker Heights High School was a part of Mrs. Friedman's social science course, "Male/Female." It began in the Spring semester of 1976–1977, and was taught by me in weekly Wednesday sessions during the first period, 8:00–8:50 A.M.. The description read:

> Mrs. Friedman's course will include one period weekly on child development, to be taught by a consulting expert in that field. Basic principles governing the growth of the personality will be discussed, showing the interaction of maturation and the facilitating environment at successive levels of development. Included are the nature and role of relationships, the development of abilities such as learning, speech, self-control, and the significance of needs, urges, and feelings. The method of teaching is by discussion and requires the students' active participa-

tion. Experience in working with children (e.g. baby-sitting, camp, nursery school), preferably concommitant with the course, is especially helpful.

Mrs. Friedman was available to discuss the course with the students at the time of course selection, adding details and my name, but none of the students had ever heard of me.

In time, these and similar formal preparatory devices were augmented by the student "grapevine" as they passed on information to each other and the child development course became an accepted and valued part of the curriculum. These formal and informal ways of preparing students have been used in various settings with participants of all ages and backgrounds. However, whereas the professionals and older parents for the most part use it to make their choice and to anticipate how the course will be conducted, a number of the high school students do not. When I asked the students in one of the initial courses how and why they had elected to learn about child development, I heard some of the following reasons, somewhat shamefacedly stated: "I really did not choose the course, it just fit into the right spot in my schedule"; "I needed another social science credit and this was the only course that suited my time"; "I really overlooked the part about the child development course and only heard about it when Mrs. Friedman told us the first day"; "I was late in making up my schedule and had to take what was still open." Quite a few of them added, "But I'm glad I did because I really like it." Indeed, most of them were particularly active and thoughtful participants. Obviously, preparation is not everything. It makes a big difference to the students' attitude however, whether they had a chance to choose and to prepare themselves or whether no such opportunity was afforded. Even the students who had missed the advance notice and learned about the child development course only at the beginning of the semester, still had the option of transferring. Thus it remains important and helpful to offer preparation to students and let them decide to what extent they use it.

3

Experiences with Teaching and Learning in the Course

A SAMPLE SEMINAR

At this point the reader is probably as impatient to know how the method works in practice as we were impatient to see the course get under way. Nothing short of actual participation can give a full picture, but the following excerpt from the first course session may convey an impression.

Mrs. Friedman had already prepared her class for the child development course. She remained in the classroom through this and all subsequent sessions, and to start with assisted in introducing each student personally.

I told the students that we would learn about child development in a special way. It may be new and hard for them but is especially suited to studying this subject. In open discussion and with everyone welcome to participate, we would think about some of the ways minds grow and, as much as possible, we would base our thinking on their observations of children. Together we would develop our ideas and explore answers to questions as they arise. Nobody need worry that they might say something foolish or incorrect because there are no simple rights and wrongs in this field. There are many ways to look at and understand each thing. We would not be able to learn everything about child development, but how much they would learn would depend mainly on how much each was willing to think hard and to contribute. I also told them about the journals and how they could be helpful to our joint work.

In order to get to know one another and to approach our first topic of relationships, we started with each student relating his or her own experience in working or being with children and we named the different kinds of relationships involved. They had been tutors, athletics coaches, camp counselors, storytellers at the children's library, baby-sitters, and some had "just been with little kids in the neighborhood" as playmates. Many belittled the importance or success of their experiences. This gave me a chance to stress that, for the purpose of understanding children's behavior and development, observations of ordinary daily events and interactions were most valuable and would prove fruitful to examine closely. It does not matter how momentous an experience is, or how well we handled it, but what makes children tick. Had not the simple falling of an apple supposedly led Newton to understand the laws of gravity?

Jenny, an intelligent, pretty young woman, told of how much she enjoyed baby-sitting because she never had trouble with the children, but what a difficult job it had been to work at Safety Town. This is a summer class for a large group of five- and six-year-olds to learn traffic rules and to help them be safe in the streets. This particular class was taught by police officers, with high school students acting as aides. "At Safety Town," she said, "there were a bunch of really obnoxious kids, crying and whining. I remember one in particular who was in tears all the time and wanted me to take him to the bathroom all the time or to get a drink. He was spoiled rotten. I couldn't do a thing to make him pay attention." What was he crying about? "He wanted his mother." Where was she? "There was a rule that the mothers could not be there after the first day." Did he have trouble the first day too? "Come to think of it, he was fine then and listened. The crying started when she dropped him off the second time. I guess, she came a bit late to get him and most of the others had gone." I sympathized with how frustrating the job had been for Jenny but wondered if she had noticed anything that would explain why the boy wanted his mother so badly or how he felt about Safety Town.

Now others began to contribute. Some had found that young children feel strange, scared, and insecure in unfamiliar surroundings. They need their mothers until they get used to new places and can trust a new person. One student told of her story group for three-year-olds at the library. When the children sat with their mothers, they were pretty quiet and attentive, but once the mothers had been asked to leave, the children had trouble. Some wanted to sit on the librarian's lap or be next to her, or they wanted her to take them to the bathroom or get drinks, others acted up, and most of them could not listen to the story. "I think it bothered them too much to be without their mothers and so they wanted attention from me rather than the story." Some mentioned that children don't like a place where they feel dropped off, and worry they'll be left there when the mother doesn't come on time. Several agreed that baby-sitters cause less upset to a young child because the child remains in his own home and the sitter provides one-to-one care similar to the mother's. In Safety Town one teacher was in charge of twenty children and could not give each child a sitter's attention. The students felt that Jenny's boy was not ready to have to share a teacher with so many others. Now Jenny herself reflected that many of the children at Safety Town looked scared but this one boy seemed quite lost and pathetic. She felt bad that she had been short-tempered with him rather than sympathetic, and then questioned whether this boy's discomfort was peculiar to him or whether perhaps Safety Town expected too much from most five-year-olds. Several students now thought that "Safety Town is a terrible place," and they recalled how shy and unhappy they had felt in new places— and sometimes still do.

Others, however, remembered how much fun they had had at camp away from their parents' strict supervision. Some baby-sitters agreed that their charges sometimes "acted up because they wanted to have fun and get away with it" rather than because they missed their parents. As the different proponents argued about whether children regard parents as protectors of their safety or as obstacles to having fun, I suggested that there was some truth in each. Perhaps it depends on certain ages or circumstances whether one or the other feeling wins out. This prompted Jenny to relate another illuminating observation. Her two-year-old niece always had a wonderful time at Jenny's home, ignored her mother, and played with Jenny, her siblings, and all their things. The toddler begged and begged her mother to be allowed to stay overnight at Jenny's home until one day the mother agreed. All went well and was much fun until bedtime came when the toddler started to cry for her mommy and would not be quieted until her mother was called and took her home. We spent some time discussing the reasons for the child's behavior, the conflict between dependence and independence, the special need for the mother at sleep time, the role of the mother in the child's bodily care.

I had, all along, underlined those ideas that touched on the nature and role of relationships and had encouraged their thinking along that line by questions: How do you know this to be so? What have you observed with children that led you to this question or conclusion? Does anyone have other observations of children in similar circumstances which provide additional or different facts? What accounts for the differences? In this session I did not contribute data or explanations. I tried to help them appreciate and muster their own knowledge and to begin subjecting it to their own scrutiny. I helped them look more closely at their observations and to relate them to their thinking. Above all, I think I helped them to put themselves in the child's shoes so that they would be able to observe not only their own reactions in a given situation but, with appropriate empathy, would be able to gauge the child's feelings and his different point of view. I did this in part through my own tolerant and sympathetic attitude toward the students' feelings and experiences ("That must have been terribly frustrating for you at Safety Town"), and in part by showing my wish to understand, rather than judge, the child's actions and by inviting the students to share my interest ("I wonder what he was crying for, I wonder why he needed his mother so badly? Do you have any idea?").

I also helped by translating parts of our discussion from the specific to the general level. This occurred mainly toward the end when I suggested that we summarize for ourselves some of the ideas and questions that had come up. We noted that their experiences and observations encompassed several very different kinds of relationships, such as teacher, baby-sitter, playmate, mother. We saw that these relationships serve different purposes—teaching and learning, substituting for the parent, providing for the child's bodily and emotional comfort, sharing an enjoyable activity. We realized that children can't maintain all these relationships right away but that one leads to the other in the course of growth. Children can relate to a sitter earlier because the sitter gives the kind of care that is similar to mother's and because the home setting is familiar, but it takes much more growing up before a child can relate to a teacher whom he has to share with many others in a new place. Many questions had arisen from these considerations: When can a child accept a teacher? How does he get to that stage? How does the mother–child relationship differ from other relationships? Are we born with an ability to have relationships? How does the first relationship begin? And what are relationships for? Do we really need them?

There had of course been many comments and questions that concerned areas of mastery and impulses: Children take a long time to get used to new people and settings. Children sometimes can't learn and can't behave when they don't feel safe and miss their mothers. What makes a child "bad"? When do children learn to behave? Isn't it wrong to spoil a child? Or, by contrast, isn't it good to let him do what he wants and when he wants? I acknowledged the validity and importance of these topics but asked the students to defer them until a later time because, to start with, we would look more closely at the beginnings of relationships in children, how they come about, how they develop and change, and what their role is.

It was an enjoyable session, with the combined advantages of some enthusiasm for its newness and some comfortable familiarity with the topic. I knew that we had "bitten off a bit more than we could chew," that some of the students' excellent observations would have to be used many times during the course to understand different facets, and that in the area of relationships our first general statements had not been understood by all. There were also several students who had contributed nothing to the discussion or whose comments revealed as yet little real thinking: "Well, kids just

want attention, that's all." Or, "Sometimes kids just act up
for no reason." Some had listened to me but not to each other,
and at least one young man had listened only to himself, and
what he had said seemed more intended to impress than to
learn.

A number of the journals following this session continued in its vein of lively and thoughtful discussion, adding
observations and some personal memories as well as more
questions, and showing grasp of concepts. Some of the best,
most detailed, and well-written journals came from students
who had not participated verbally in class, showing that they
preferred this form of learning and communicating at this
time. But others contributed as little in writing as they had
orally. A few considered the class session introductory and
missed out on what we had learned. They could not empathize with the child, could not grasp the significance of the
everyday observations, and could not follow the step from the
specific to the general.

There were as yet no personal questions to be taken up
individually and the general questions raised in the journals
overlapped with those we had stated for ourselves at the end
of the first session. I therefore planned to begin the second
session with a closer look at the functions and origins of the
mother–child relationship. Such progression from one topic
to the next, in keeping with the syllabus outline, is possible
when the class discussion and journals indicate the students'
potential readiness. There is, however, also an ongoing paral-
lel cyclical approach. Some topics, or aspects of them, crop up
prematurely and are explored more deeply at later points;
others reappear in different contexts and require repeated
discussion although considerable time was devoted to them
earlier. For example, the children's wish to have fun (to grat-
ify their impulses) without parental interference was largely
shelved at the beginning. Later, when we worked on inner
controls and, much later again, when urges were under discussion, we understood the children's wishes better; but this,
in turn, afforded new insights into the nature of the
parent–child relationship which we had studied in some detail before.

UTILIZING THE METHOD

Some topics are taken up in almost every session, especially those which concern the skills connected with this method of teaching and learning, and the teacher–student relationship which provides the milieu for the joint work.

Observing

Improving the students' skills in observing is an ongoing task. Their main difficulty with it usually arises from the fact that they do not value their own ability to observe, do not value the situations they have a chance to observe, and often do not value children. They tend to feel that observing is a specific scientific laboratory skill, spelled with a capital O, which some professionals use, equipped with stopwatch and notepad, but which is not a tool everyone, especially they, can use. It is often a new idea for them to realize that observing simply requires interest, effort, and the good use of one's own senses and thinking, and can be an enjoyable activity. In the same vein, many assume that only momentous unusual events are worth observing; "What happened when you baby-sat for your neighbor's little girl?" "Nothing. Nothing special happened. It went all right." It is often a new idea that the fact that it did go "all right" is a remarkable phenomenon, well worth observing in the greatest detail to ascertain how this came about, what the child, sitter, and parents contributed to its success, and whether it was a success not only from the adults' but also from the child's point of view. The difficulty in valuing children often shows, for example, in that the student is then likely to recall from the baby-sitting experience what the adults did and said, leaving out the child's part, as though the child were a thing manipulated by the grown-ups, not a person whose thoughts, feelings, and means of coping were as important or could make as good sense.

The teacher helps, of course, by encouraging and appreciating the students' observations, valuing them, exploring details, and using them to illustrate points or to raise new issues. Above all, the teacher helps by being a good observer, enjoying observing children, and by bringing observations from everyday life, from situations accessible to all, in the neighborhood, in stores, in buses, to alert students to all the golden opportunities that constantly surround them. For example, my account of a short-lived ball game I happened to pass in the street near my home, led to a lengthy discussion of the ways in which young schoolchildren use rules imposed by their conscience and rules imposed by others, by the game, the parents, and the community. It also led to students bringing many of their observations of children playing games. Observations have to be an integral part of forming and applying concepts. The teacher's emphasis on linking general ideas to observational data in whatever he or the students present, also helps to make observing a focus of the work. It often prompts students to recall what they have observed and to utilize it newly in their thinking. Some teachers have also used additional means of stressing the importance of observation and of improving the students' skills with it. They have, for example, required a certain number of written observations or given extra credit for them. One teacher used a short film of a family interaction to discuss with the students after the showing what they had observed or missed.

On the whole, however, films, tapes, and pictures are not helpful aids in teaching observation or, for that matter, in teaching child development as such. Even when they portray natural rather than staged and acted events, they represent the selected view of others without affording us the opportunity to question them. When a teacher or student relates an observation, we can ask him or her to clarify the context or to furnish more details, and can in this way evaluate the data, either come to a fuller understanding, or pinpoint gaps and inconsistencies. The audiovisual aid prohibits this, allows us only a specific circumscribed view, chosen by the unknown unavailable author. The extent to which we can learn from another person's observation also depends on how close it lies to our own knowledge of the subject. In order to integrate it effectively, it has to be fairly close. This is always less likely to be the case when the observation comes from an unfamiliar outsider. The maker of a film, for example, is in that sense an invisible, distant guest speaker. We do not know him and he does not know us. For these reasons it generally holds true that the best chance for observing a baby is to take care of it oneself, the next best is to be with a mother who is taking care of her baby, and the least helpful is to see a movie of a baby, however expertly filmed.

Concentrated Thinking

A topic that also requires repeated discussion is the concentrated thinking necessary for learning and teaching in this course. In spite of the teacher's helpful initial explanation and warning of its difficulty, students may not really understand or appreciate how hard it is until they have several sessions of experience. This may show in less conscientious journals or failure to hand them in, or in diminished participation in discussion. Among the refreshingly frank high school students it may also show in requests for the teacher to give lectures or show movies, in suggestions for role-playing or other games, instead of thinking, and in an outright wish to forego learning because a class precedes or follows a vacation period, or because it is too hot or cold on a particular day. One student even wanted to devote an occasional lesson to a coffee-and-doughnut party!

It helps to pick up these signs and to devote some time to discussing the method, exploring the students' objections and reasons for their various suggestions for alternate methods, recognizing the hardship of the demands, and relating their ideas to their wish for learning in this course and their understanding of learning in general. This also gives those students a chance to speak up who find this method particularly congenial or productive, at least at times, so that varied viewpoints can be compared. In one such discussion an honors student and rather active participant in the course described his experience:

> In twelve years of schooling I have never worked so hard as in this course. In calculus, in history, in English, in fact in every other course, I pay attention for ten minutes, then I goof off, then I concentrate again and pick up what

I missed, or I look it up in the textbook later or ask a buddy for his notes. In this course, if I goof off I can't pick up what was said and I can't look it up in the textbook later or ask a buddy for his notes. And if I ask someone for his notes I know that they don't tell me anything because what he got out of the discussion is bound to be different from what I would get out of it. So I have to concentrate the whole time, for the whole period, week after week, and it's darn hard and I'm not used to it. But I've learned a lot.

Another student, with an average academic record, felt very differently. I quoted her earlier: "When you are first asked to figure out your own answers you sort of feel you can't do that and you don't know what to think or say. But once you give it a go, it's really so easy and it all comes so naturally, like finding the pieces of a puzzle and suddenly it all fits. It's fun." Most students find this way of learning sometimes easy and sometimes difficult, depending on their personalities and on the topic under discussion. But it is true that many young people, and many older ones, have not acquired the skill of concentrating for a class period of fifty minutes or even less, although their school day has been subdivided into such time segments for several years. Nevertheless, when they are helped to recognize this difficulty and supported in overcoming it in order to achieve their learning goals, many try and increasingly succeed, in part through practice and in part because the inherent rewards they feel spur them on.

Although I have offered my students genuine sympathy with their struggles, I have not accepted their suggestions for alternate, less demanding, and less effective methods, nor have I arranged for breaks in learning or parties. Through our talk students become more aware that they not only want to "take it easy" but also want to learn as much as possible about child development, that they and I share this goal, and that they expect me to do my best to help them reach it. Such discussions usually lead to thoughts and questions about the nature and rewards of learning, the use of tests and grades, the role of the teacher–pupil relationship, the developmental achievements which underlie the capacity for learning, in short many of the topics pertaining to child development and contained in the course syllabus.

Difficulties with the method may, at times, also reflect a student's inner obstacles to coping with the feelings around certain topics. For personal reasons, a student may find it hard to address one or another aspect and this may show in withdrawal or boredom, in chatting with a neighbor, in coming late, or missing a session, in "fighting" an issue, or the teacher, or in objecting to the way it is taught. The teacher may, in these instances, acknowledge that we feel differently about different parts of the material, that some aspects are harder than others, for each of us, and that perhaps the next or a later topic will prove more interesting or more understandable. Of course, individual students' temporary difficulty may also be related to events and experiences in their lives outside the child development course. These the teacher does not know about and can neither assess nor alleviate. However, when all or most of the students bring objections or cannot learn well at a certain point, it is possible that the teacher either presented some material in a way that bothered them or that the class discussion of it got out of hand and impinged too strongly on the students' feelings. Every teacher makes mistakes. As long as he finds them, apologizes for, and corrects them, they need not create a lasting interference. For example, when the class described in the sample seminar, much later discussed masturbation in young children, I mentioned that this is often a difficult subject for people to talk about because it is such a private matter. This attempt on my part to make the topic less threatening did not succeed. A number of students showed their discomfort by relating rather provocative observations, unintentionally shocking others as perhaps they had been shocked, and several expressed it in a reproach against me, "You misjudged us. We are mature people and we don't mind talking about these things. What you said sounded like you were talking down to us." I simply apologized and learned to introduce the topic in a more tactful way, better suited to their developmental stage.

Different Ways of Learning and
Mastering Concepts

At the same time that students object to the difficulty of the method, they often do not appreciate how successful they are in utilizing and mastering it. In the absence of the customary tests and grades, they do not know how to gauge their efforts. They blame themselves for not contributing enough to discussions or for not writing lengthy journals, or for not knowing *the* answers, and they fail to recognize and allow for the fact that each person learns best in his or her own way. This not only includes varied preferences for written or verbal expression and varied ability to address some topics with inner ease and to shy away from others, silently withdrawing from them or defensively attacking them. It relates mainly to the different manner in which individuals approach and integrate ideas and master and apply concepts. The teacher has to learn how each student goes about it, support the students own means, and sometimes offer additional ones. With the teacher's patient encouragement and never lagging expectations, many students grow in their ability to think and learn. Sometimes they gradually gain confidence, at other times, perhaps in connection with a certain topic, they may suddenly come alive and experience a significant spurt in their learning. Some students may need to reject an idea repeatedly before they can thoughtfully consider it, others are eager to adopt new concepts but then take a long time to "digest" them and make them truly their own.

A student's form of expression, through talking or writing, is not as indicative of his progress as the steps he takes toward mastering concepts. The following means of dealing with ideas illustrate some of the ways in which students take such steps, which enables the teacher to gauge their progress and to assist them with it:

The ability to look at unfamiliar ideas and to consider the views and experiences of others that are at variance with his own; for example, in the session described above, the "argument" as to whether children miss their mothers as protectors or view them as obstacles to impulse gratification showed that some of the proponents on either side could contemplate the other's opposing view and apply their thinking to it, while others had to reject outright what was not strictly in accord with their own ideas. The teacher's ability to listen to and consider the students' different viewpoints, as well as his or her tolerance for the manner in which they present them, serves as a helpful model and often enables others to follow suit.

The ability to grapple with new concepts; for example, during that same argument it became evident that some of the students' doubting and opposition did not represent a rejection of the unfamiliar ideas but an attempt to struggle with them in order to facilitate integration at a later point. Obviously, the teacher needs to respect such attempts and must not mistakenly interpret them as insults or rebellion.

The ability to think from the specific to the general; this was exemplified by those students who recognized that the stress of Jenny's Safety Town boy represented all young children's concerns when they face new situations alone. Although this step often has to be taken by the teacher, it is most helpful when he or she can merely "set the stage," perhaps by asking, "Do you think this tells us something about all children? And if so, what?" and inviting the students to formulate the concept.

The ability to think from the general to the specific; this was illustrated by Jenny's observation of her toddler niece in response to my general statement that a child's wishes for dependence and independence coexist and that different stages and circumstances evoke one or the other side of that coin. This is one of the ways in which students apply concepts, an important step in mastery. It is often introduced by them with "This reminds me of when. . . ."

The ability to sift the important from the ancillary; this was demonstrated by the student who recognized that, in her library story hour, the three-year-olds' various behaviors represented different reactions to the basic cause, namely the absence of their mothers. Finding the causal factor, or common denominator, of varied observed behaviors and experiences is a most helpful step in thinking, one the teacher always looks for, facilitates, and sometimes has to contribute himself.

The ability to learn with one's total personality, utilizing both intellect and feelings; for example, when Jenny came to empathize with her Safety Town boy, she also recognized and felt her own anger and pity for him, and formulated the idea that certain situations impose unmasterable demands on children and on those who care for them. Although it is difficult to encourage such learning directly, the teacher's ability to use feeling and thinking appropriately with the students and the subject helps indirectly.

Making the step from preconscious to conscious knowledge, from vaguely sensing it to actually knowing it; this, I believe, occurred when the library storyteller, in recalling her experience, realized that her three-year-olds' loving of her as well as their badgering demands had the same aim, namely to secure her in a one-to-one relationship.

Sometimes students feel radiantly happy or deeply satisfied with such a new insight or step in understanding, but often they neither know nor appreciate these important stages in their own learning. When the teacher points them out, students may gain assurance, courage to work even harder, or genuine relief. This was especially brought home to me with one young woman. I commended her for her serious efforts in grappling with new ideas because she often learned by arguing with my statements and bringing contradictory evidence, which was her way of confronting within herself old and new knowledge. She was surprised at my praise. She had feared that her behavior might not be becoming for a good, obedient pupil. She had failed to think of it as her way of learning. Yet, the teacher's contributions are meant to be tested and there is a real difference between a student's provocative argumentativeness and his intense struggle with unfamiliar ideas.

Obviously, this method is as demanding of the teacher as

it is of the student. It requires full concentration and effort, during the class sessions, in reading the journals, in thinking through what has transpired, what to take up next, how to correct the mistakes one made, how to respond to individual students' questions or difficulties, and how to extend the limits of one's own knowledge. Most teachers, like their students, however, find the hardships worth struggling with for the sake of the satisfactions gained. And teachers, as well as students, sometimes tell us that their gains for their own teaching and learning are as helpful as what they learn about child development.

Everybody has his or her weak spots and limitations. The successes, hardships, and occasional failures with this method are for the most part related to a student's individual personality rather than to his or her intelligence, academic proficiency, or other qualities. In our classes, at the Shaker Heights High School and the School on Magnolia, were students of both sexes, of different races, religions, socioeconomic status, and of varied cultural and ethnic backgrounds. There were honors students, average learners, and a considerable number with severe learning problems and with such limited intellectual functioning that they were placed in special classes with alternate study programs in most subjects. We found a similar, though less wide range, among the parents and professionals we worked with. These variations did not correlate with a student's ability to participate and learn. They did of course affect a student's ways of expressing himself, the specific observations brought, and values held. The few who seemingly could not be helped to learn much (though we can never be sure of that) appeared handicapped by factors within their personalities. They included some who were known to be very bright in other subjects as well as some who could not apply themselves in any area. Likewise, very active learners in child development sometimes were good at everything and sometimes had not progressed beyond the elementary school level in other subjects.

Creating a Milieu for Learning

At several points we have already discussed how the teacher creates an environment in which the cooperative goal-directed work with the students can proceed as productively as possible, and how he or she minimizes potential interferences: for example, how the teacher builds an individual relationship with each student through classroom discussion and through reading and commenting on the journals; how he prepares the class for the work, considers and discusses the students' ideas and responses, encourages their ways of learning, and sympathizes with their hardships, but maintains expectations and trust in their ability to improve and master; how he conveys his own enjoyment of the subject and the learning process and invites them to share it, instead of offering them immediate gratifications of respites, games, or cookies to compensate for the "chore" of working; how he steers and contains the discussions to avoid inappropriate tangents and to assure that everyone's contributions serve learning; how he takes care to foster the continuity of the joint work by taking up thoughts, questions, and misunderstandings which had arisen in the discussion or journals relating to the preceding seminar; and how he offers, rather than imposes, his own observations and understanding.

Although these and other aspects of the teacher's role came up in different contexts, I hope they allowed the general underlying emphasis on respect to emerge; respect for the subject matter, for children, for learning, and for the students. When we talked about the manner in which Mr. Wiehe helped his class to make use of Mrs. Machlup's presentation, his good "mothering" was mentioned, but this simile was not intended to compare the students to preschoolers but to point out that *good* mothering implies the highest and most thoughtful respect for another person and is an essential ingredient in all our relationships. In the child development course, the teacher's respect for the students is especially important, in part to facilitate their active participation in the work, in part to help them respect children. The following incident illustrates this. It happens in many classes that outsiders want to visit. On two occasions social workers became interested and actually joined the class for the entire semester, learning with the high school students, enjoying it, and profiting from it. More often, a parent, professional from another field, teacher, or reporter want to attend one session.

Regardless of whether the class consists of high school students, professionals, or parents, and regardless of how long or often the guest wants to attend, the teacher always discusses such a request first with the students, explains who the guests are, why they want to come, and how long they wish to stay, and obtains their permission and stipulations. In practice no class has ever refused to admit a guest (although I would abide by their decision if it were soundly based) but students have sometimes set conditions, such as "Ask him not to take part in the discussion (or ask him to sit in the back) so that his presence does not get in the way of our work." This paid off when in one such class, one of the high school students offered to bring in her three-month-old nephew to let the class see how well he was developing, as this topic was then being discussed. The teacher wondered how the baby would like that and reminded the class how they were consulted about strangers coming to "look at them and see how they are getting along." This helped others in the class and eventually also the young woman to recognize that the baby's feelings have to be respected too, that we cannot ask him and let him judge for himself, but may assume that it may be upsetting for him to be in strange surroundings and to be watched by a whole group of unfamiliar people. They also guessed correctly that the baby's bahavior would be affected by the stressful circumstances and would not provide a good opportunity for observation.

Respect for the students' personal feelings and experiences also guides the teacher's presentation of the subject matter and discussion of comments and questions at all times. We can never know for sure what individual students have lived through or how they feel about it but their questions about "a friend" or about "someone I know" and their occasional comments in journals or in a few moments of private conversation with the teacher have shown that no group of students lacks personal tragedies and deprivations, however composed and unaffected they may appear. Among our students were victims of rape, incest, and aggressive abuse, their families included delinquents, convicted criminals, drug addicts, alcoholics, and psychotics. Some knew assault, murder, and violent strife, repeated parental abandonment, changes in foster care, suicide and bereavement, not to mention divorce, adoptions, and unwed mothers, in short the whole gamut of human afflictions.

Keeping this in mind does not imply that such topics should be avoided or "soft-peddled," but it does mean that the teacher has to be tactful in discussing them and has to make sure that he conveys his respectful, compassionate understanding for people with every kind of misfortune or pathology, that he regards them as "Us," not as "Them."

Often enough, upsetting events occur in all schools, involving perhaps students other than in the course, which cast their pall over the entire student body and preoccupy everyone's thoughts. Among the tragedies we encountered during recent years were students suiciding, two students murdering a third one, drug abuse leading to personal disaster, delinquencies and vandalism, sexual and aggressive assaults on students in the vicinity of the school, and threatening gunmen entering the school building. It is realistic, respectful, and helpful to address such incidents in a way that enables the students to cope sufficiently and then frees them for resumed learning. This means neither to ignore the events and the students' feelings nor to become involved in an excited discussion of all the details, rumors, and speculations. If a student does not raise the issue, it is best for the teacher to do so at the start of the session. Sometimes it suffices to say, "I heard about what happened. I am very sorry for all who were actually involved and I am also sorry for the upset, scare, and sadness it has caused everyone in the school. I am sure it bothers you as it bothers me." Students may then be able to get on with their work, or may, for example, question the nature of the person's pathology who commits crimes or of one who fails to keep himself safe. If this relates to topics that have been discussed, such questions may be clarified. Students usually feel most upset and threatened when they think that what befell another could have easily happened to them or been somehow caused by them. Sometimes this concerns safety measures which may be reviewed. Most often it concerns unexpected suicides. Here it always helps to discuss the special mental illness and long-standing difficulties that lead to suicide, and which can be treated only by a professional. It also needs to be stressed that suicides are not caused by recent disappointments or by anyone's unkindness, and that there is a big difference between wishing one were dead, which all of us wish sometimes, and actually killing oneself. One such class discussion was concluded by a young woman saying with great relief, "I guess I could never really do it. I just like myself too much."

Not infrequently, we learn of our students' own stressful experiences and have to decide how to respond in the most helpful way. At least once during each child development course a student undergoes a current upset, such as the death of a parent. If the student tells us about it privately, a few words of genuine sympathy suffice. If the teacher learns about it from others and ascertains that it is a matter of common knowledge, he may write a brief note of condolence and place it on the student's desk before the next seminar, to convey sympathy, yet spare the student a perhaps unwelcome conversation. Sometimes students bring their past personal experiences or long-standing difficulties to the teacher's attention. They may do so in their journals or in private conversations, to which the teacher responds with a brief, sympathetic verbal or written comment. Students usually appreciate the appropriateness of the teacher's simple acknowledgement of and empathy with their misfortunes or predicaments and close the issue. If the teacher does not stay within these limits, inherent in the teacher–student relationship, the student's capacity to learn with him may be jeopardized. This could happen if the student's concern were altogether ignored or if it were to evoke a degree of personal involvement befitting a family relationship, friendship, or therapeutic contact. Teaching and learning can only be satisfying and rewarding in a setting where feelings and worries are neither totally shut out nor allowed to take the center of the stage. The teacher's attitude helps to maintain a proper balance. Many students can then devote themselves to learning in spite of their distress and even find some relief and respite in it.

There are occasions when students "spill" their concerns, leave themselves no room for learning, and invite the teacher's help or participation with their personal lives. They may fill a journal with their emotional account in lieu of answering its questions or, very rarely, introduce some of their troubles in class discussion. In these situations the teacher speaks with the student privately, expresses sympathy, and, if need be, suggests that he or she may wish to get assistance from the school social worker or other mental health professional. But the teacher also points out that it is best for everyone to use the course only for learning about child development and to refrain from sharing private concerns because this does not make one feel good in the long run and may disturb the work of the rest of the class.

When a student's difficulties manifest themselves in behavior which is inappropriate in the classroom, the teacher also needs to help to restore the learning milieu. Whether and how to address these situations will depend on the nature and cause of the difficulty and on the extent to which it interferes with the work of the class. Some students, especially at the start of the course, worry about their presumed inadequacy. This may manifest itself defensively by showing off— wearing garish clothes, swaggering into the classroom at the last moment, giggling or chatting with neighbors, relating silly experiences, making categorical statements about children and educational methods, or contradicting everything others say. The fact that such behavior makes the teacher feel inferior, foolish, or unworthy helps him to recognize that such are the student's own underlying feelings and enables him to respond by attempting to raise the student's self-esteem through the work, especially by considering and appreciating any constructive contributions and disregarding the inappropriate ones. As such students come to feel more confident in their learning and sense that the teacher will not belittle them but offers a respectful relationship, their manners usually improve.

When the difficulty continues for a long period, the teacher may speak to the student about it privately. For example, one young man repeatedly brought out a big cartoon sheet, poured over it rather conspicuously, and did not participate in the discussions. The teacher told him after a Friday class that it seemed he had difficulty with this course, perhaps the material gave him trouble. The student appar-

ently mulled this over all weekend and came to the teacher
first thing on Monday saying that it was hard but he really
wanted to try and do better—and he did. A measure of provoc-
ativeness in high school classes is often related not only to
difficulty with the material (and helped by pointing this out)
but is also inherent in the adolescent rebellion. When it does
not affect the tenor of the class too much its main danger lies
in inducing the teacher to respond in kind. As long as he
remains unruffled and respects the young people's need to
assert their individuality, even if that implies their being
contrary, things usually can be contained within manage-
able bounds. If the behavior interferes too much with the
student's own learning it may be helpful to mention this to
him, lest he forget this important aspect during his one-sided
fight against "authority." "You have been needing to fight so
much. It's a good thing to stick up for one's ideas but it seems
to get in the way of your learning more new things. I don't
think you'd want to lose out on that."

Occasionally a student is characterologically argumen-
tative or provocative in his behavior, may make himself the
focus of the class, and even attract a following among peers.
His difficulty then interferes with the learning of all. It can
also easily turn into a battle for power with the teacher,
reducing the latter to the same toddler level, and spoiling the
chance of regaining a more mature working relationship
with the class as a whole. The moment the teacher becomes so
irritated that he allows himself to be drawn into the struggle
and takes measures to "make" the student behave, he has in
fact joined in the trouble. If private discussion of the fact that
the difficulty interferes with the student's own and others'
learning bears no fruit, it may be necessary to ask him to
leave the class, temporarily or permanently, because it is the
teacher's responsibility to protect all students' right to learn.

The teacher's proper handling of any of these difficulties
does not necessarily produce immediate results and may not
affect the very disturbed student at all, but it always helps the
other students, allows them to take a more mature attitude,
and often serves as the best, though not specifically identi-
fied, example for later discussions on discipline and
punishment.

4

Evaluating Progress and Achievement

We face serious obstacles whenever we try to evaluate, not to mention measure, human attitudes, knowledge, and behavior, and attempt to gauge how and why they change and whether such changes are beneficial. Education is but one of the fields dogged by these perennial, inherent difficulties. Even in basic areas of learning there has been ongoing controversy about how to assess pupils' progress and achievement in mastering content, how to correlate these with attitudes to learning and methods of teaching, and how to know whether the student's performance in school does or will bear a relationship to his ability to use his knowledge later and to apply it in other areas. Few educators feel that grades provide adequate answers to these questions, and fewer yet trust that tests do. With the subject of child development the obstacles to evaluation are much greater. Our study group gave this much thought.

Since learning child development is not a purely intellectual skill but involves all aspects of the student's personality, mastery of concepts varies individually in nature, extent, and pace. Some may integrate concepts during the course but many do not integrate them until much later; some may grasp aspects of several concepts, others may select a few but understand them much more fully; some may know a concept, be able to define and describe it but be unable to use it, others may use it but not know it in general terms. Application of concepts, a very important aspect of mastery, is especially likely to manifest itself later, in one or more areas. Equally important indicators of the students' progress are their attitudes to the material and ways of learning it, and their use of observational skills. These pave the way for continued learning later and for application. They are, however, just as individual and dependent on personality factors and do not readily lend themselves for comparison between students. The method we use actually maximizes each student's individual contribution to how, when, and what, or to what extent, he learns, because it is purposely geared to help students utilize what their personalities bring with them and to develop and understand better what they already know and feel. We have no way of measuring or gauging what a student brings with him at the start of the course. We can at best assume that the interest in child development is related to factors in their own personalities but this tells us nothing about their nature. Some may be capable because they are in touch with their feelings and can easily achieve insight; others may be particularly flexible during a current phase of personality development and therefore able to effect marked realignments of inner forces; and others yet may have a special capacity for integrating new models and ideas. But there may be many who lack most of the functions and skills for this kind of learning. No report card from a previous grade level can tell us what a student already knows and how capable he is in learning this subject. As mentioned earlier, the students' learning abilities and achievements in other courses do not correlate with their aptitude and attitude to learning child development.

In our courses for professionals and parents we have therefore generally tried to assess for ourselves individual students' initial abilities and skills as well as areas of progress and achievement during the course. We have done this by attending closely to their observations of children, their written and oral contributions, manner of participation in discussions, comments showing whether, what, and how they are gaining understanding and integrating new ideas, and how they are beginning to apply them in their professional or parenting work with children. We also listened carefully to the students' spontaneous remarks about how they felt about the course, what they thought they learned, what they considered helpful or unhelpful in applying it to their work with children, and/or other areas. We did not grade or give report cards but merely certified that a student had taken the course if he or she had an attendance record of at least 75 percent.

We sought a more meaningful assessment through long-term follow-up. Many of the professionals and parents indeed continued working with us for several years and many others remained in contact through professional associations, through visits and letters, and through meetings at workshops and conferences. In addition to these informal opportunities for collecting data we have also used yearly form letters, asking past course participants whether and how they may have continued to utilize what they had learned. It was primarily through these later comments that we learned how much they valued the understanding they had gained and how often they applied it to furthering their professional growth and to appreciating parenting, in themselves and in others. The only formal follow-up study involved nursery school teachers (Redmond, 1979).

In instances where students used our courses for college or postgraduate credit, such as master's degrees in education, health sciences, and related fields, it was necessary to grade their work. Mostly we tried to mark it pass/fail, based on attendance. When a specific grade was required, it was my custom to arrange a conference with the student to compare his prepared self-evaluation with my assessment and to discuss discrepancies before handing in a final grade. Students usually underrated their own achievements.

In evaluating the high school students' work we faced a different situation. Long-term evaluation would be difficult if not impossible, and short-term evaluation would need to include grades or their equivalent.

We considered follow-up studies but decided against them. The fact that most high school seniors leave town after graduation and take up very different lines of work over the years, allows but rarely for informal continued contacts and makes it impractical to reach them. Occasionally students have returned for visits or encountered a former teacher by chance. When this happened they referred appreciatively to what they had learned in the course and sometimes detailed how they felt it had helped them. One young woman credited her ability to cope with an especially stressful parental bereavement to what she had gained. But these instances are too few and too selective to warrant general conclusions. Criteria for formal follow-up studies, such as were used with nursery school teachers, would be difficult to develop since they could not focus on application in professional work. Also, the intensive methods necessary to obtain meaningful data could not be used because they require a considerable amount of time and cooperation from the subjects. It would not seem proper or helpful to impose such procedures on past students and to intrude into the privacy of their personal growth and perhaps much later parenting.

Having to forego the more desirable long-term evaluation, we focused on short-term assessment during the course. We decided to follow as closely as possible the students' contributions to the discussions and their written journals to obtain data about the areas which had proven significant for purposes of assessment: observational skills, approaches to and means of learning, mastery of concepts, and ways of applying them. We also hoped that special attention to spontaneous comments about any aspect of the course would allow potential new areas of assessment to emerge and that, as part of a wind-up session at the end of the course, we would invite students to think over what, if anything, they had gotten out of the work and to share their ideas with the teacher. During the first three courses, taught by members of the study group, we made detailed notes after each session and journal reading and, as I described, indexed them for each student and under the expected and newly emerging unexpected headings. In going over the data we learned a good deal about the students' learning processes and were often surprised at their approaches to and use of the material. Later courses, taught by the recently trained teachers, were not documented in the same meticulous fashion. Instead, regular meetings with the teachers served to discuss their notes and to pool and compare their experiences. Over several years, these studies both confirmed and extended our initial tentative conclusions.

ASSESSING THE STUDENTS' PROGRESS IN MASTERING CONCEPTS AND SKILLS

Although I shall attempt to group our findings under several headings, such divisions are inevitably artificial because observation, steps in learning, and integration of concepts in thought and practical application usually coincide, and more often than not form an organic whole. Discussion of them will therefore overlap and repeat certain themes.

Observational Skills

I have earlier detailed the students' difficulties in observing and the teacher's unremitting effort to assist them in improving their attitude and skills. Increased attentiveness to people, and especially to children, and greater accuracy in observing them tend to go hand in hand with the most important change—a change in attitude. Students' observations become much less judgmental and much more thoughtful, empathic, tolerant, and at the same time more objective. When this begins to take place their interest in observing increases too, they attach more value to it, and to what they and others observe, and they are better able to use it in their thinking. They reevaluate past experiences and apply what they have learned to understanding and handling new observations.

Jane M.'s occasional anecdotes from baby-sitting revealed a somewhat harsh, domineering attitude to children. As she became more sympathetic to her charges, she related the following observation: A toddler visiting from a South American country tried to teach her Spanish. She tolerated his relative bossiness with good humor because, as she said, she guessed how overpowered and stupid he would often feel when everyone tried to teach him English. She thought he needed a chance to turn the tables for a while. After some discussion of this in the class, she reflected that this helped him later to cooperate with her necessary demands on him and enabled them to get along well.

Tom K. who coached baseball with a group of eight-year-olds, had complained about their aggressiveness and carelessness with equipment. Later he reported on a boy who "looks like he has trouble with anger and can't even seem to help it." The boy would suddenly shout out loud and attack others without provocation.

Helen T. wrote in her journal: "I have often had good and bad experiences with baby-sitting. I never knew why things sometimes went smoothly and sometimes were a struggle from start to finish. I have thought over each of them and found that the difference comes perhaps from whether the parents prepared the children or suddenly took off when I arrived. I now ask parents to tell the children ahead of time and to stay and tell them and me all that has to be done. It works out much better."

The teacher always focuses his own and the students' observations on children in younger age groups, does not bring observations about his own person or family, and refrains from discussing his observations of the students as individuals or as a group. By contrast, despite the teacher's model, many students make their families, friends, and themselves the subjects of *their* observations. This may be due to the fact that such observations are easily available, but observing others also involves a measure of self-observation. These "close to home" observations are rarely reported initially. Perhaps students are too reserved at the start, but perhaps such observations only become possible when the student has become more accepting of what he sees.

Susan B. thought about this in her journal after some weeks of struggling successfully with her difficulty in learning to use her own resources instead of "just taking notes of what the teacher says": "For myself, I have found that many things I observe in children are pertinent to my own life experiences and what they do often comes back to me. I know that this course is not supposed to be analyzing the individual, but to understand children one also has to delve a little deeper and see the child in oneself."

It has seemed that this use of consciously available memories and experiences has furthered rather than impeded integration. Late adolescence is a time when many people feel the necessity to recapture memories of early childhood, to reevaluate them from a new perspective, and to fit them into new contexts.

Steps in Learning

The students' difficulties with concentrated thinking and with developing their own ideas and integrating new ones were discussed earlier, and a number of specific steps in learning were described. In that connection we also discussed the many ways in which the students' learning depends on their ability to establish and use the teacher–pupil relationship appropriately and on the teacher's ability to foster the cooperative goal-directed work and to create in the class a milieu for learning.

Students' ways of learning do not always follow these well-known paths, however. The individual nature of a student's learning may not even show itself unless he happens to let us know or responds to our question about it. With Jim B. I noted repeatedly that he had really mastered a concept, was not merely parroting it, but I still don't know how he went about it. Barbara H. was always silent during discussions but her journals showed that she had understood all that was said, and more, and she often concluded her written comments with penetrating questions. When I once answered one of these questions in a little talk with her before the start of the session, I asked her why she did not participate in our discussions since she obviously had so much to contribute from which all of us could learn. "I am much too busy taking it all in. I can't talk at the same time. Then later I go over it and over it in myself and then it all fits in and then I can write what I think about it."

Perhaps the most striking and often evident way of learning child development is not via thinking but via feeling, the "intuitive" self-evident certainty of knowledge philosophers used to talk about. Sometimes it is accompanied by insight ("Aha, it clicked"), sometimes by bodily gestures, sometimes it is just suddenly there. The following examples illustrate these ways:

During a discussion of toddlers' love–hate relationships with their mothers, Marie S. suddenly blurted out, "Ah, now I know what it is when two people who are close fight all the time. They just haven't gotten over their toddler days."

In talking about early mothering, some students asked whether the biological mother can be replaced by another mothering person. Before I had a chance to respond, Fran C. made a spontaneous gesture covering her abdomen as though she were pregnant and said; "But of course it's easiest and best when the mother cares for her own baby because it's a part of her own body." I might add that many young women responded in the same immediate way to this topic.

Gary W. commented in his journal: "What you said about the baby crying at an unfamiliar face I know was true but I have never been with a baby. I just know it."

Forming and Applying Concepts

The teacher frequently has the opportunity to witness a student's manner of grasping a concept and connecting it with a recalled observation or experience with others or with an insight and understanding of himself.

We were discussing the role of words in helping us to think in logical sequences. Amy S. referred back to two observations she had shared several weeks earlier: While baby-sitting, one boy ran around naked in the living room. She took him gently to his room and suggested he get dressed if he wanted to be in the living room. Another boy she baby-sat for was naked in his bed, which she noticed when she bid him good-night. When he looked at her questioningly she told him it was his room and he could be naked when private. When I used her examples at that time to illustrate the "not here but there" principle used in the education of drives, she was astonished: "But I just did it. I didn't know what I was doing with those boys." Now she took it up again and added: "I know why I didn't know what I was doing with those boys.

I had never thought it out in words. But now I know and that's how words help."

The same young woman helped herself to understand how drives can interfere in learning. She related it to her observations of children in the nursery school where she worked part-time. "That's just what happens when during a story some children suddenly ask questions that have nothing to do with what is going on, or want to sit on my lap, or start poking another child."

Jason M. addressed the same concept of drives interfering in learning. He related it to peers and, with some justification, to himself, and did so in the relative privacy of his journal: "I don't know about little kids but I have witnessed people not doing well because they're showing off. I guess I have sometimes done it too. The only thing that is accomplished is that others think you're immature and you just may flunk the subject."

Her journal showed that Connie C. struggled with the concept of mother–father–child for several weeks. She first tried to relate it to her baby-sitting experiences with a fatherless child, then to her much younger sister who, since her parents' divorce, had not received the benefit of the father's presence in the home. She went on to discuss it thoughtfully with each of her parents and finally wrote, "I was very lucky to have both my parents together for many years. It's important."

Joan V. contributed to our discussion of the progressive changes in children's pleasure-seeking activities: "I have noticed that the children at the nursery school stop messing with paints when it becomes more fun for them to have a nice picture appreciated."

Our records show that many students apply their understanding to the subject matter of the courses, such as Criminology and Male/Female, which include the child development seminars and they also utilize it in thinking about other topics. During the seminars the teacher learns mostly about applications of concepts to the work with children or younger siblings. The examples above, like the Spanish-speaking toddler, the request that parents prepare their children for the sitter, and others illustrate this. Sometimes the students report only their puzzlement but cannot as yet integrate thinking and doing.

Terry J. worked several hours weekly in a residential home for convalescent children. She writes in her journal: "The younger ones always ask me for candies and hugs and some just take it out on me because I substitute. I know they miss their families but I don't know what to say to them."

Of course, not all students show progress and achievement in learning during the course. The marked individual variations in all aspects of the process make it difficult to draw comparisons. The teachers feel that some classes are predominantly "with it" and "just take off," that in others the majority experience ongoing difficulties, and that others yet indicate a bell curve distribution. The factors responsible for these differences sometimes include the teacher's varying investment in the work, a succession of school events interfering in the continuity of the seminars or preoccupying the students' thoughts, or a particularly fortunate or unfortunate composition of the group.

On the whole, however, our findings over the years warrant the conclusion that the students can and do learn what we intended to teach them about child development and that they learn it in the manner we try to facilitate.

HOW THE STUDENTS USE THE COURSE AND ASSESS WHAT THEY LEARN

In studying the students' approaches and responses to the material and in listening to their spontaneous and solicited comments on what they have valued about it, we learned to our surprise that what is most important and meaningful to them differs from what we specifically aimed for and indeed never directly addressed.

Earlier I mentioned that one of these areas is learning itself. Many students and teachers tell us that what they have come to understand about teaching, learning, and the teacher-pupil relationship outweighs their increased knowledge about child development as such and has been immensely useful to them, personally and in their work with others. We know from our work with the teachers over the years that they have modified their attitudes and techniques in their courses in all subjects, although they were excellent teachers to start with. They have, for example, increasingly fostered appropriate teacher–pupil relationships and cooperative goal-directed work. They have focused more on helping students recognize their own goals, and their wish to work toward them and meet them. They have encouraged students to evaluate their own work and attitudes, have pointed out interferences, and urged them to overcome them because they, the students, want to succeed and feel good about themselves. They have also felt that they could better understand individual students and handle their difficulties with learning and behavior more successfully without becoming unduly involved.

Since we have no long-term follow-up, we do not know whether the students who felt they had got so much out of our work on teaching and learning have actually utilized their understanding. We hope it has served them in some measure.

The second and much more prominent area is parenting. It is the male and female students' main focus of observation, learning, and mastery. It is the area in which we found the most evident progressive changes in their attitude, and it is the topic most of them singled out in their spontaneous and solicited comments on what they got out of the course. Many students realized that they viewed themselves as potential parents. Many came to appreciate the role of the parents in their own and others' lives. Many talked with their parents about topics discussed in the course and questioned them about their ideas and experiences. Many felt that the course had made them more understanding of their parents and brought them closer to each other, and many commented that what they had learned had changed their ideas about the ways they would parent.

The following vignettes illustrate these points:

Viewing Self as Potential Parent

After a seminar on the role of the mother substitute, Lisa K. wrote in her journal: "If I were younger it would have been very helpful to understand more about what a baby-sitter's role is. But now that I'm older the parent–child relationship seems to hit closer to home."

In relation to the topic of meeting a baby's needs, Anne R. noted in her journal; "I found it fascinating. I'm not sure if that is because I am a woman and a someday mother or if it is just interesting. Do you know how men respond to that?" (She obviously was not thinking of the "boys" in her class whose responses she had heard, but of "men" in the future.)

Ginny S. wrote on the role of the mother–child relationship; "For me who will be a mother it was surprising and meaningful to see that mothering can determine the whole outcome of a human being, from growing and taking care of oneself to having sexual relations with others."

Kevin W. wrote, after a discussion of the father–child relationship, "I think it is very important that fathers take an interest in their young children and play with them, even if they are not home much. That's what I will do when I am a father."

Appreciating Own and Others' Parents

In commenting on identification, Donna A. writes: "It was meaningful to me that when children love a person they want to become like them. I thought in how many ways I am like my parents and how many things I must have loved and admired them for. It is something I was unaware of but yet I experience it daily."

On the role of the father Melissa Z. writes: "I know how much it means to a girl to have a loving father. One of the girls I sit for has divorced parents. She is always all excited when she gets to visit her father. I took my father for granted yet when I think back I remember all the lovely times we had."

On the topic of early mothering Betty writes: "I am glad to understand more about how important and hard mothering is, which I may some day do myself. I never realized that my mother did all that."

George N. writes on expression of anger: "I get so mad at

my Dad and we often have arguments. I always think if only he could see I want to be a person in my own right. But I guess I only begin to see how hard it is to be a parent."

Trina B. commented on the question of how parenting relates to being parented: "I have seen parents who let their child have everything she wanted because they were kind of making up to her what they did not have. But they did not make their daughter happy because they were really pleasing themselves."

Henry S. contributed to the discussion on developmental levels; "I think people should wait to be parents until they are sure they are mature enough to have a child and have really grown up themselves."

Students Talking to Their Parents

Diana W. wrote after a discussion on neonates: "I asked my mother how she felt since she has given birth to four children. She told me that after going through the pain in giving birth and bringing a life into the world there could be no one else who could love the child more."

Beth J. discussed her adoption with her mother and told us: "I am adopted and I sometimes thought that was a bit hard for me but now I thought it would have been hard for my mother. I asked her and she agreed and told me how scared she was because she had so little time to get ready."

Karen T. had been very defensive about physical punishment, insisting that it is necessary for parents to hit their child if he does not do as told. She later reported that she had questioned her mother about it and she had said that it's impossible always to be patient when there is a big family but perhaps if there is only one child a parent would not have to hit. Karen was very thoughtful.

David S.'s father had grown up as an orphan. At one point David S. had complained about how his father never understood any fun and always pressured him to work. Later he mentioned he had asked his dad about his experiences and had realized how hard it had been for him: "He had a tough life and never had much fun himself."

Laura M. often talked with her mother about course topics and asked her to visit a seminar, which the mother actually did. The mother told Laura and me afterwards how meaningful the class had been to Laura, how much Laura had learned about parenting, and had come to see "what life is really about," and how it had brought them closer in a new way.

Jessica T., whose parents were divorced and who had thought a lot about the effect of this on her younger siblings, reported talking with her mother about how hard parenting was, and asking her how she did it singlehanded. They had a long, warm talk about it in which the mother apologized for her shortcomings. According to Jessica, her mother very much wanted to sit in on one of our sessions but could not get off from work.

Although the students not infrequently report discussing the course with their parents, the teacher usually does not have contact with the parents. Occasionally an open house has provided such an opportunity during which quite a number of parents expressed their appreciation. In all the years, only one set of parents objected to the course. Although their son did rather well in his work, they disagreed with the teacher's views on some of the topics

Changing Ideas on Parenting

Laura V. stated in her journal: "I always thought I'd go right back to work after I have a baby, but now I think it's so important to be with one's baby I will definitely take out a long time from work."

Missy H. thought: "I always believed that children's thumb sucking and other infantile habits have to be suppressed with threats and punishments. I would now aim to help my child channel some of his body pleasures into other outlets."

John H. noted: "I can well see that it would be hard to parent if one had a lack oneself. But I was lucky and have a good chance to be a good father—if I work hard at it."

Ellen M. was in a quandary: "A child deserves complete attention and a parent has to do all he can to give them all they need. But I think it's hard to work out being concerned with raising children and having a need for an individual life unrelated to children."

What Students Feel They Learned

Trina B.: "I learned the most important thing ever and that's how important it is to be a parent. It'll be enough even if I forget everything else."

Tim N.: "I didn't know how much one's life depends on one's parents, how much they have to care."

George N.: "I understand now what being a father is all about."

Ginny S.: "Parenting and how hard it is and how much one has to put into it and how much one can get out of it."

Walter C.: "I never knew parents did so much, and how important it is."

Needless to say, the theme of parenting was not in the foreground with all students. Whether and to what extent their interest focused on it, may be determined by the particular point students have reached in their own development and by their individual life circumstances. In light of the overall interest, however, we concluded that what the course perhaps does best is to help students understand, in a new way, what parenting is about and to look at their own and others' parents, not as a child might, but as prospective parents themselves. Perhaps this will play a part in how they parent.

GRADES AND REPORT CARDS

How can one translate such evaluations, and their related uncertainties, into grades? Yet grades are often required in school settings and our customary certificates of attendance or pass/fail mark cannot readily be substituted. Since the work is too individual to grade students on their learning processes and mastery of specific concepts, it has seemed most helpful to use as a basis for grading, the criteria of attendance, timely completion of oral and written assignments (journals and reports on observations), and attentive effort. If, and only if, a grade has to be given, the teacher discusses with the students exactly how many points or percentages are assigned to each of these "measures," so that the students can, at all times, gauge which grade they are earning for themselves. The teacher encourages them to keep an eye on their achievement during the course to avoid last minute surprises. (One of the teachers related that he responds to the students' questions of, "What grade will you give me?" with, "The question really is what grade are you giving yourself.") In one school, comments and checks in areas of effort and task completion took the place of grades. This made it less specific but equally important to appraise students of how the teacher evaluates their participation. When child development courses are included in another course, some teachers inform the students that their grades will depend only on their work in the other subject, and that child development is a completely ungraded course.

Absence of grades, or absence of grades for the real course work of thinking and learning, does not imply absence of evaluation. The teacher keeps a close eye on each student's work, assesses all aspects of it, gauges ways of supporting progress and of helping to overcome interferences, and notes all changes. This all-round, ongoing evaluation provides a much more accurate basis for understanding a student's progress, or lack thereof, than a list of checks for isolated specific achievements. Hand in hand with the teacher's evaluation of the student's work goes his or her responsibility of helping students to evaluate their own work. At different points I have described how the teacher assists students in recognizing and valuing their ways of learning and their contributions of ideas and questions as well as how he helps students, in private conversation, to look at their difficulties in learning or behavior. The busy school schedule and large numbers of students leave little time to focus on students' self-evaluations. It helps to remind ourselves that they may learn more from assessing their work than from packing in yet another bit of subject content. It has been our experience that the absence of achievement grading has not made students lazy or disinterested. On the contrary, in many instances it removes an untoward pressure and enables them to devote themselves to learning more freely and effectively. Even some of those who claimed that people only work for grades, demonstrated through their active discussion of and thinking about this topic how interested they were. They often recognized that learning has many other motives and that learning well or poorly affects our opinions of ourselves, though we may prefer not to notice.

5

Who Can Teach Child Development

Although our study group initially shelved the question of what it takes to teach child development and focused instead on the role of the student, we knew all along that we ourselves would not be able to teach the course indefinitely. Its continuation and availability to more students would depend on our helping others to take over. With this in mind, we looked for teachers who were interested in the subject and worked in a school which would be willing to incorporate the course in the curriculum and which provided a good learning milieu, in our terms. After careful exploration we were particularly fortunate to find Penny Friedman at the Shaker Heights High School. She was not merely interested in the subject but more than fulfilled our other requirements. She was a skilled teacher, whose record of excellent and dedicated work over many years was greatly respected. Well versed in the basics of teaching social science and in tune with her students' educational needs, she had successfully introduced a number of innovative changes in the syllabus and felt strongly that child development, although outside her field of expertise, would interest many students and benefit their all-round education for life. Through her efforts and enthusiasm, she was able to enlist the helpful cooperation of members of the administrative staff at all levels and to interest her equally competent and experienced colleague, Theodore Wiehe, in joining our pilot project. Both teachers knew from the start that a member of the study group would do the teaching first

65

and that we would broach the question of their teaching when all of us had more practical experience with the course.

Since the first three consecutive child development courses were included in Mrs. Friedman's "Male/Female" social science course for seniors, she sat in on all weekly sessions during the three terms taught by Dr. Robert A. Furman and myself. She also read all the students' journals and met with the child development teacher almost weekly to coordinate efforts, to assist in the compilation of data for our research, to gain better understanding of the work, and to discuss her own questions about it. Halfway through the second term she expressed her wish to teach the course herself and asked our group to plan a training that would prepare her sufficiently for such an undertaking. Mr. Wiehe was similarly interested. He had not participated in the students' course but had kept in close touch with Mrs. Friedman who had shared her experiences. Both teachers hoped that we would find others with like interests to participate in their learning.

In the light of our own experiences with teaching the course, the study group had, by this time, repeatedly discussed our qualms about whether it would really be possible for others to do this work. Someone skilled and experienced with traditional methods of teaching would have a helpful background in classroom management, but would he be able to make the change, learn our method, and make it successfully enough his own to put it to effective use? Without long-term professional training in child psychoanalysis and child development, would he be able to master the contents sufficiently to understand the students' responses to the material, to deal with their questions, and to handle the discussions? On the other hand, if someone were a child psychoanalyst and expert in child development but had no training and experience as a teacher, would he not encounter just as much of a handicap in teaching this course? The very few who combine professional background in both fields may not be interested in giving this course or may not have access to a suitable setting elsewhere. Obviously, we were asking for the impossible.

WHAT THEN ARE THE ESSENTIALS AND HOW CAN WE BEST WORK TOWARD ACHIEVABLE GOALS?

To become an effective teacher of this child development course, a person has to have a real feel for children, practical experience in dealing with them, and a strong interest in their emotional development. He or she has to have an ability to kindle such an interest in the students, and has to enjoy sharing with them in a cooperative learning effort. This includes respect for the students and for learning, as well as an appreciation of the inner rewards of learning and working. These enable the teacher to devote the necessary effort and energy to the task and to support the students in doing the same. Given these basics, prospective teachers could then begin their actual training by taking the child development course themselves, to learn the content and method. How much and what kind of further help teachers would then need, we would gauge step by step, in consultation with them, and learn from experience.

Mrs. Friedman and Mr. Wiehe had the "basics." In addition, they had a very fine professional background in teaching and in education in the wider sense, and had demonstrated their flexibility in using different methods of teaching without neglecting the necessary emphasis on effort and hard work or sacrificing the goals of learning. In exploring with others who might meet the same basic criteria, we were again very fortunate in finding Marilyn Machlup and Carl Tuss who had learned about the child development course through my consultative work with them at the School on Magnolia and who were eager to introduce and teach it there as part of the curriculum. Their board supported this plan, and the school setting, geared to students with special learning needs, seemed appropriate. In addition, Mrs. Machlup is a trained teacher and Mr. Tuss worked several years in other schools as educator and social worker. Both are qualified nonmedical child psychoanalysts. Although they held administrative positions as principal and assistant principal, they also taught a number of courses at the school.

This group of four prospective teachers enrolled in the spring of 1978 in a course on child development which followed exactly the content and method of the high school students' course which was then in its third semester. They met with me eleven times in weekly one-and-a-half-hour evening sessions which often extended to two and more hours, in part because the discussions were so lively, and in part because we also spent time on preparing for their classroom work which was to begin that fall. Mrs. Friedman took on four child development courses in her several classes and Mr. Wiehe took on two in his. He also regularly attended one of Mrs. Friedman's classes to familiarize himself with the teaching techniques which Mrs. Friedman had had so much more opportunity to observe. Both teachers taught several child development courses again in the second term of that academic year. Mrs. Machlup's first class did not begin untill the spring term and Mr. Tuss followed later. The teachers from the School on Magnolia were better acquainted with the practical aspects of our method because they had themselves participated in other such courses on related topics and had used it, in adapted form, to meet the special needs of some of their students. Throughout this first year of their teaching, the teachers continued their course with me on a now two-weekly basis. This period of work no longer followed the sequence of the course syllabus. Selected topics related to content were brought up by the teachers as they noted gaps and uncertainties in their knowledge or came up against new aspects through their students' questions and comments. Our discussions served to extend and deepen their understanding of the material and made them feel more confident in talking about it in their classes. At times, I as seminar leader or Dr. Rich, as recorder–assistant, pinpointed and clarified areas of misunderstanding and introduced pertinent additional aspects of a topic.

The teachers had anticipated that they would not know the answers to many of the students' questions and we had discussed ahead of time two ways in which they could handle this. When a difficult question comes up, they could tell the students that they, the teachers, did not know the answer but would think about it and take it up in the next session, using the interval to consult with us (we were always available for "emergencies"). Alternatively they could tell the students at the start that they were consulting with an outside specialist in the field who would help with questions that they could not answer. The teachers decided "to level" with the students and told them at the start. This did not present a problem and did not interfere with the teacher–student relationship and work.

During that year's seminars with the teachers, much time was also spent on discussing the use of the method: presenting material in helpful ways (interesting but not exciting); techniques for helping skills in observing (such as the role of the teacher's model); guiding discussions (focusing topics, discouraging misuse of words); responding to individual questions, commenting on journals, creating a learning milieu, and coping with interferences, in short many of the topics discussed in the preceding chapters. Even during their first year the teachers were not spared upsetting events, among them a suicide which required class discussion with the students.

While the students fared well and learned enthusiastically for the most part, the teachers were often full of misgivings and doubts about their competence and needed encouragement and well-deserved appreciation. They worked very hard and found it exhausting. In time though, we all recognized how much they had gained and by the end of the year all were eager to continue teaching. They felt they were truly integrating the contents, were truly utilizing the method of teaching and learning, could begin to apply their understanding in the course work with the students and in other areas, and experienced a sense of mastery.

During their second year of teaching, they requested that we meet monthly. The discussions now focused less on content and method and more on understanding individual students' difficulties in learning and behavior, and on ways of helping them. Increasingly the teachers took the initiative in devising their own techniques for supporting the students' learning, for coping with difficulties, for evaluating and grading. At one school hundreds of students had now taken the course; at the other school the numbers were small but there had been more opportunity to experiment with a younger age group, with more disturbed children, and with different frequencies of seminars. Mrs. Machlup and Mr. Tuss were also teaching the course outside the school to groups of professionals and parents. These multiple experiences provided us with many fascinating observations on all aspects of the work. Together we sifted through them and gained new insights and understanding. Much of what we learned has been included in this text. At the same time, the teachers began to use completed chapters which made their work easier.

By the summer of 1980, after two-and-a-half years of study, four experienced skilled teachers in child development were working with students.

In the subsequent three years, we remained available for consultation but had planned meetings only twice each term to discuss the progress of our work, teaching experiences, continuing research data, and a number of practical problems, among them changes in high school curricula and requirements. At one point these problems threatened the continuation of the course at the Shaker Heights High School, and the cessation of the School on Magnolia as an independent entity in the summer of 1982 ended the child development course there but freed its teachers for more course work with different groups, such as adolescent unwed mothers and infant care workers.

These years also served to evaluate our teacher training program. All felt that it had been adequate and successful. We concluded this not only from the facts that the teachers were confident and satisfied with their work, that the students learned and benefited, and that our observations confirmed their reports, but we took into account a number of other indicators which we considered especially significant:

1. There was evidence, from the teachers' statements and from our observations in meeting with them, that they wanted to and indeed did continue to learn, to deepen, and integrate their understanding and to apply it ever more effectively. The aftereffect of our method was at work. Their own observations, thinking, and experiences and those of their students served the ongoing process of learning more on their

own. This left no room for complacency or for getting stuck in a rut. They noted new gaps in knowledge, were intrigued by new and different questions and responses from their students, and were alert to interferences or difficulties. They approached these challenges thoughtfully, utilized them to gain deeper understanding, to reevaluate, and, if indicated, to alter their handling. On the one hand this made their work hard, harder than in other courses they taught, on the other hand it afforded them much pleasure and satisfaction; as some put it, "I feel I've grown and go on growing."

2. They increasingly valued their work and its importance for the students. This prompted them in one school to expend much personal effort and time and to leave no stone unturned to assure the future continuation of the course at a time when new regulations threatened to interfere in the years ahead. This was likewise evident with the teachers in the other school who were unable to continue their work there, but immediately explored and found other settings where they introduced the course and taught different groups of students. It would have saved them all a lot of trouble if they had simply bowed to the seemingly inevitable and had discontinued teaching.

3. It is important to keep in mind that the teachers were not paid for their training, devoted only their private time to it, and did not benefit financially from including the child development course in their work. This speaks, of course, to their special character qualities but also bears testimony to the continued interest the course had kindled in them and to the satisfactions they derived from their learning and work.

It is striking how closely the work with and by the teachers parallels our experiences in teaching other professionals who do not go on to teach child development but apply their knowledge to their work with children and parents in other capacities. The usual sequential steps leading to mastery are:

1. The initial child development course.
2. A year or more of requested two-weekly seminars which no longer follow a planned curriculum but are of a

consultative nature, in the sense that the students bring their own topics for discussion, focused on their work experience and suited to their pace of integration.

3. Continued learning, characterized now not only by mastery of concepts and increased facility in applying them, but also by initiative in self-learning. During this period students rely on working with a consultant at longer intervals. They use him or her to help clarify some aspects but they also teach the consultant new aspects which become available through their observations and work experiences, and derive from their thinking. Students and consultant now learn from and teach each other more equally and join efforts in exploring and understanding phenomena new to both.

Misgivings and doubts about their own competence invariably accompany all such learning, and students always find it tiring, even exhausting, to look at perhaps familiar experiences in a new light, to appreciate new aspects hitherto unexplored, and to struggle with frustrating hurdles in understanding. This is especially true during the earlier phases of their work, but to some extent remains a part of it, not only in learning and teaching child development but in most things we work at. Nor do these hardships entail only negatives. They also indicate that we continue to realize how much we don't know and are actively engaged in figuring it out. This provides some special pleasures and satisfactions too. How boring it would be to come to a point in one's work, or for that matter in life, when one would feel that one has seen it all and knows all about it, when one has lost all sense of wonder, does not seek new vistas nor wishes to view old ones from a new vantage point, when a new experience no longer challenges one to explore and puzzle over it and to devote effort toward understanding it a bit better.

Fortunately, this is not the only enjoyment the work brings a student of child development at any time in his or her learning. All along there are the satisfactions gained from new understanding, from increased mastery and ability to apply them in one's work and other areas. There are also inner rewards experienced in furthering one's pupils' learning and often, though not always, in seeing them grow and earning their appreciation.

CAN THIS TRAINING BE MADE AVAILABLE TO OTHERS WHO WANT TO TEACH CHILD DEVELOPMENT?

We have thought about and discussed this question. Undoubtedly there are persons with the basic essential qualities who are interested in learning to teach this child development course. There also are, no doubt, academic and other settings with a suitable learning milieu and with innovative and helpful administrators. There certainly are many students able and willing to learn about child development and to benefit from doing so.

Are there experts who could teach the initial course to prospective teachers? Yes, there are. It would be possible for members of our Center to teach a course during the summer semester, in which prospective teachers from this and other areas could participate with little or no interference in their usual work. It would also be possible to organize such a course in several other geographical locations, where persons with special skill and experience in child development, education, and child psychoanalysis reside. For example, preliminary inquiries indicate that a number of child psychoanalysts with expertise in education, in teaching, and in consulting with teachers are keenly interested in this work, especially as the availability of this book as a guide and source makes the task less arduous for teachers and students.

Where would prospective teachers observe the course being taught? This would present a problem, but perhaps not an insurmountable one. Among our four teachers, only one had extensive opportunity to observe a course for high school students in action. One observed a colleague in training and two had only some similar prior experiences. The chance to see others teach is no doubt helpful. The most important experience in this respect, however, is the prospective teacher's own participation in the initial course, the model of the teacher who teaches him or her, and the teacher–student relationship they develop in the process. The ongoing work with a consultant may then suffice to assist the teacher when he begins classroom work.

Who would teach the later "consultation" courses when

the new teachers begin their practicum? A local consultant would need to undertake this work. If the initial course took place in the area where the new teachers work, they could continue with the same consultant. If they attended the initial course elsewhere, a new local expert would have to work with them. It is essential to have ongoing opportunity for extended learning, for help in applying it to one's own teaching, and for discussing practical aspects of class management. Interested consultants with sufficient skill and experience are not everywhere available. This imposes a definite limitation on teacher training.

Who will bear the cost of training? It is unlikely that all teachers and all consultants will always give of their time without monetary compensation, but it is likely that, given the motivation of self-elected interest, they will expect their main rewards to be professional and personal rather than financial. Big outlays are not required, small expenses may be covered from operating funds and special grants.

We have learned that interested teachers of child development show extraordinary perseverance and resourcefulness. They may persuade reluctant administrators, may track down consultants, and find ways of traveling to seminars, may raise funds or even pay out of their own pockets. Where there is a will, there is almost always a way.

CAN THIS BOOK SERVE AS A SUBSTITUTE FOR THE TRAINING WITH A TEACHER?

I do not know—yet. I wrote this book in part because I thought it likely that many who currently teach child development with a similar approach to the material will be able to use its content chapters and will also wish to learn and use the method we found so helpful. If their teaching rather closely approximates the one described here and if they are good self-learners, they may well be able to use this book as their teacher–consultant, at least to a "good enough" extent. If their teaching methods have been rather different, they may, with the help of this book, be able to integrate some aspects of the "new" method or adapt others to fit their framework of teaching. It may also be advantageous for the students to use the book, not only as a source for contents but as a guide to the method, so that they can understand better their part and can join the teacher in his efforts. At the same time, the teacher would benefit from the assistance of a consultant, perhaps at less frequent intervals than we used.

However, novices who have not taught child development on similar lines before and who bring to their studies only the basic qualities listed above, would do best to use this book in conjunction with the training program we outlined.

IS IT POSSIBLE TO USE THE CONTENT CHAPTERS OF THIS BOOK IN CHILD DEVELOPMENT CLASSES CONDUCTED ALONG TRADITIONAL LINES?

Yes, it is possible to use the material without using the method. A more traditional child development course may be structured around the content chapters, or it may serve the teacher as a guide and source book, or it may be used as one part of a course syllabus. However, without the use of the method to facilitate the work, both teaching and learning will be less effective and less satisfying.

References

Furman, E. (1978) Use of the nursery school for evaluation. In: *Child Analysis and Therapy*, ed. J. Glenn, New York: Aronson, pp. 129-162.

———— (1980), The death of a newborn: Assistance to parents. In: *The Child in His Family: Preventive Child Psychiatry in an Age of Transition*. Yearbook of the International Association of Child Psychiatry and Allied Professions, Vol. 6, ed. E. J. Anthony & C. Chiland, New York: John Wiley & Sons, pp. 497-506.

———— (1981), Helping children cope with dying. In: *Social Work and Terminal Care*, ed. L. H. Suszycki, A. H. Kutscher, & D. Fisher. New York: Praeger, 1984, pp. 15-23.

———— (1984), *Mothers, Toddlers and Care*. In: ERIC, ED 256 479, Urbana, IL: University of Illinois at Urbana-Champaign, 1985. Also Pamphlet Series of the Cleveland Center for Research in Child Development, 2084 Cornell Road, Cleveland, Ohio 44106

———— (1986), *What Nursery School Teachers Ask Us About: Psychoanalytic Consultations in Preschools*. Madison, CT: International Universities Press.

Furman, R. A. & Katan, A. (1969), *The Therapeutic Nursery School*. New York: International Universities Press.

Redmond, S. L. (1979), *Evaluating the Child Study Group: Psychoanalytic Consultation with Preschool Teachers. A comparative Study*. Unpublished doctoral dissertation. Department of Education, Case Western Reserve University.

Index

79